YOUTH

Also by J. M. Coetzee

Dusklands
In the Heart of the Country
Waiting for the Barbarians
Life & Times of Michael K
Foe
White Writing
Age of Iron
Doubling the Point: Essays and Interviews
The Master of Petersburg
Giving Offense
Boyhood: Scenes from Provincial Life
The Lives of Animals
Disgrace
Stranger Shores: Essays 1986–1999

YOUTH

J. M. Coetzee

VIKING

VIKING
Published by the Penguin Group
Penguin Putnam Inc., 375 Hudson Street,
New York, New York 10014, U.S.A.
Penguin Books Ltd, 80 Strand,
London WC2R 0RL, England
Penguin Books Australia Ltd, 250 Camberwell Road, Camberwell,
Victoria 3124, Australia
Penguin Books Canada Ltd, 10 Alcorn Avenue,
Toronto, Ontario, Canada M4V 3B2
Penguin Books India (P) Ltd, 11 Community Centre, Panchsheel Park,
New Delhi – 110 017, India
Penguin Books (N.Z.) Ltd, Cnr Rosedale and Airborne Roads, Albany,
Auckland, New Zealand
Penguin Books (South Africa) (Pty) Ltd, 24 Sturdee Avenue,
Rosebank, Johannesburg 2196, South Africa

Penguin Books Ltd, Registered Offices:
Harmondsworth, Middlesex, England

First American edition
Published in 2002 by Viking Penguin,
a member of Penguin Putnam Inc.

10 9 8 7 6 5 4 3 2 1

LIBRARY OF CONGRESS CATALOGING-IN-PUBLICATION DATA
Coetzee, J.M., 1940–
    Youth / J. M. Coetzee.
        p. cm.
    ISBN 0-670-03102-X
    1. South Africans—England. 2. London (England).
    3. Young men. I. Title.

PR9369.3.C58 Y68 2002
823'.914—dc21   2002016879

This book is printed on acid-free paper. ∞

Printed in the United States of America

Wer den Dichter will verstehen
muß in Dichters Lande gehen.
                     – Goethe

ONE

He lives in a one-room flat near Mowbray railway station, for which he pays eleven guineas a month. On the last working day of each month he catches the train in to the city, to Loop Street, where A. & B. Levy, property agents, have their brass plate and tiny office. To Mr B. Levy, younger of the Levy brothers, he hands the envelope with the rent. Mr Levy pours the money out onto his cluttered desk and counts it. Grunting and sweating, he writes a receipt. 'Voilà, young man!' he says, and passes it over with a flourish.

He is at pains not to be late with the rent because he is in the flat under false pretences. When he signed the lease and paid A. & B. Levy the deposit, he gave his occupation not as 'Student' but as 'Library Assistant,' with the university library as his work address.

It is not a lie, not entirely. From Monday to Friday it is his job to man the reading room during evening hours. It is a job that the regular librarians, women for the most part, prefer not to do because the campus, up on the mountainside, is too bleak and lonely at night. Even he feels a chill down his spine as he unlocks the back door and gropes his way down a pitch-dark corridor to the mains switch. It would be all too easy for some evildoer to hide in the stacks when the staff go home at five

I

o'clock, then rifle the empty offices and wait in the dark to waylay him, the night assistant, for his keys.

Few students make use of the evening opening; few are even aware of it. There is little for him to do. The ten shillings per evening he earns is easy money.

Sometimes he imagines a beautiful girl in a white dress wandering into the reading room and lingering distractedly after closing time; he imagines showing her over the mysteries of the bindery and cataloguing room, then emerging with her into the starry night. It never happens.

Working in the library is not his only employment. On Wednesday afternoons he assists with first-year tutorials in the Mathematics Department (three pounds a week); on Fridays he conducts the diploma students in drama through selected comedies of Shakespeare (two pounds ten); and in the late afternoons he is employed by a cram school in Rondebosch to coach dummies for their Matriculation exams (three shillings an hour). During vacations he works for the Municipality (Division of Public Housing) extracting statistical data from household surveys. All in all, when he adds up the monies, he is comfortably off – comfortably enough to pay his rent and university fees and keep body and soul together and even save a little. He may only be nineteen but he is on his own feet, dependent on no one.

The needs of the body he treats as a matter of simple common sense. Every Sunday he boils up marrowbones and beans and celery to make a big pot of soup, enough to last the week. On Fridays he visits Salt River market for a box of apples or guavas or whatever fruit is in season. Every morning the milkman leaves a pint of milk on his doorstep. When he has a surplus of milk he hangs it over the sink in an old nylon stocking and turns it into cheese. For the rest he buys bread at the corner shop. It is a diet Rousseau would approve of, or Plato. As for clothes, he has a good jacket and trousers to wear to lectures. Otherwise he makes old clothes last.

He is proving something: that each man is an island; that you don't need parents.

Some evenings, trudging along the Main Road in raincoat and shorts and sandals, his hair plastered flat by the rain, lit up by the headlights of passing cars, he has a sense of how odd he looks. Not eccentric (there is some distinction in looking eccentric), just odd. He grinds his teeth in chagrin and walks faster.

He is slim and looselimbed, yet at the same time flabby. He would like to be attractive but he knows he is not. There is something essential he lacks, some definition of feature. Something of the baby still lingers in him. How long before he will cease to be a baby? What will cure him of babyhood, make him into a man?

What will cure him, if it were to arrive, will be love. He may not believe in God but he does believe in love and the powers of love. The beloved, the destined one, will see at once through the odd and even dull exterior he presents to the fire that burns within him. Meanwhile, being dull and odd-looking are part of a purgatory he must pass through in order to emerge, one day, into the light: the light of love, the light of art. For he will be an artist, that has long been settled. If for the time being he must be obscure and ridiculous, that is because it is the lot of the artist to suffer obscurity and ridicule until the day when he is revealed in his true powers and the scoffers and mockers fall silent.

His sandals cost two shillings and sixpence a pair. They are of rubber, and are made somewhere in Africa, Nyasaland perhaps. When they get wet they do not grip the sole of the foot. In the Cape winter it rains for weeks on end. Walking along the

Main Road in the rain, he sometimes has to stop to recapture a sandal that has slipped free. At such moments he can see the fat burghers of Cape Town chuckling as they pass in the comfort of their cars. Laugh! he thinks. Soon I will be gone!

He has a best friend, Paul, who like him is studying mathematics. Paul is tall and dark and in the midst of an affair with an older woman, a woman named Elinor Laurier, small and blonde and beautiful in a quick, birdlike way. Paul complains about Elinor's unpredictable moods, about the demands she makes on him. Nevertheless, he is envious of Paul. If he had a beautiful, worldly-wise mistress who smoked with a cigarette-holder and spoke French, he would soon be transformed, even transfigured, he is sure.

Elinor and her twin sister were born in England; they were brought to South Africa at the age of fifteen, after the War. Their mother, according to Paul, according to Elinor, used to play the girls off against each other, giving love and approval first to the one, then to the other, confusing them, keeping them dependent on her. Elinor, the stronger of the two, retained her sanity, though she still cries in her sleep and keeps a teddy-bear in a drawer. Her sister, however, was for a while crazy enough to be locked up. She is still under therapy, as she struggles with the ghost of the dead old woman.

Elinor teaches in a language school in the city. Since taking up with her, Paul has been absorbed into her set, a set of artists and intellectuals who live in the Gardens, wear black sweaters and jeans and rope sandals, drink rough red wine and smoke Gauloises, quote Camus and García Lorca, listen to progressive jazz. One of them plays the Spanish guitar and can be persuaded to do an imitation of *cante hondo*. Not having proper jobs, they stay up all night and sleep until noon. They hate the Nationalists but are not political. If they had the money, they say, they would leave benighted South Africa and move for good to Montmartre or the Balearic Islands.

Paul and Elinor take him along to one of their get-togethers, held in a bungalow on Clifton beach. Elinor's sister, the unstable one he has been told about, is among the company. According to Paul, she is having an affair with the owner of the bungalow, a florid-faced man who writes for the *Cape Times*.

The sister's name is Jacqueline. She is taller than Elinor, not as fine-featured but beautiful nonetheless. She is full of nervous energy, chain-smokes, gesticulates when she talks. He gets on with her. She is less caustic than Elinor, for which he is relieved. Caustic people make him uneasy. He suspects they pass witticisms about him when his back is turned.

Jacqueline suggests a walk on the beach. Hand in hand (how did that happen?) in the moonlight, they stroll the length of the beach. In a secluded space among the rocks she turns to him, pouts, offers him her lips.

He responds, but uneasily. Where will this lead? He has not made love to an older woman before. What if he is not up to standard?

It leads, he discovers, all the way. Unresisting he follows, does his best, goes through with the act, even pretends at the last to be carried away.

In fact he is not carried away. Not only is there the matter of the sand, which gets into everything, there is also the nagging question of why this woman, whom he has never met before, is giving herself to him. Is it credible that in the course of a casual conversation she detected the secret flame burning in him, the flame that marks him as an artist? Or is she simply a nymphomaniac, and was that what Paul, in his delicate way, was warning him about when he said she was 'under therapy'?

5

In sex he is not utterly unschooled. If the man has not enjoyed the lovemaking, then the woman will not have enjoyed it either – that he knows, that is one of the rules of sex. But what happens afterwards, between a man and a woman who have failed at the game? Are they bound to recall their failure whenever they meet again, and feel embarrassed?

It is late, the night is getting cold. In silence they dress and make their way back to the bungalow, where the party has begun to break up. Jacqueline gathers her shoes and bag. 'Goodnight,' she says to their host, giving him a peck on the cheek.

'You're off?' he says.

'Yes, I'm giving John a ride home,' she replies.

Their host is not at all disconcerted. 'Have a good time then,' he says. 'Both of you.'

Jacqueline is a nurse. He has not been with a nurse before, but received opinion is that, from working among the sick and dying and attending to their bodily needs, nurses grow cynical about morality. Medical students look forward to the time when they will do night shifts at the hospital. Nurses are starved for sex, they say. They fuck anywhere, anytime.

Jacqueline, however, is no ordinary nurse. She is a Guy's nurse, she is quick to inform him, trained in midwifery at Guy's Hospital in London. On the breast of her tunic, with its red shoulder-tabs, she wears a little bronze badge, a casque and gauntlet with the motto Per Ardua. She works not at Groote Schuur, the public hospital, but at a private nursing home, where the pay is better.

Two days after the event on Clifton beach he calls at the nurses' residence. Jacqueline is waiting for him in the entrance hall, dressed to go out, and they leave at once. From an upstairs window faces crane down to stare; he is aware of other nurses glancing at him inquisitively. He is too young, clearly too young, for a woman of thirty; and, in his drab clothes, without a car, plainly not much of a catch either.

Within a week Jacqueline has quit the nurses' residence and moved in with him in his flat. Looking back, he cannot remember inviting her: he has merely failed to resist.

He has never lived with anyone before, certainly not with a woman, a mistress. Even as a child he had a room of his own with a door that locked. The Mowbray flat consists of a single long room, with an entryway off which lead a kitchen and a bathroom. How is he going to survive?

He tries to be welcoming to his sudden new companion, tries to make space for her. But within days he has begun to resent the clutter of boxes and suitcases, the clothes scattered everywhere, the mess in the bathroom. He dreads the rattle of the motor-scooter that signals Jacqueline's return from the day shift. Though they still make love, there is more and more silence between them, he sitting at his desk pretending to be absorbed in his books, she mooning around, ignored, sighing, smoking one cigarette after another.

She sighs a great deal. That is the way her neurosis expresses itself, if that is what it is, neurosis: in sighing and feeling exhausted and sometimes crying soundlessly. The energy and laughter and boldness of their first meeting have dwindled to nothing. The gaiety of that night was a mere break in the cloud of gloom, it would seem, an effect of alcohol or perhaps even an act Jacqueline was putting on.

They sleep together in a bed built for one. In bed Jacqueline talks on and on about men who have used her, about therapists who have tried to take over her mind and turn her into their puppet. Is he one of those men, he wonders? Is he using her? And is there some other man to whom she complains about him? He falls asleep with her still talking, wakes up in the morning haggard.

Jacqueline is, by any standards, an attractive woman, more attractive, more sophisticated, more worldly-wise than he deserves. The frank truth is that, were it not for the rivalry between the twin sisters, she would not be sharing his bed. He is a pawn in a game the two of them are playing, a game that long antedates his appearance on the scene – he has no illusions about that. Nevertheless, he is the one who has been favoured, he should not question his fortune. Here he is sharing a flat with a woman ten years older than he, a woman of experience who, during her stint at Guy's Hospital, slept (she says) with Englishmen, Frenchmen, Italians, even a Persian. If he cannot claim to be loved for himself, at least he has been given a chance to broaden his education in the realm of the erotic.

Such are his hopes. But after a twelve-hour shift at the nursing home followed by a supper of cauliflower in white sauce followed by an evening of moody silence, Jacqueline is not inclined to be generous with herself. If she embraces him at all she does so perfunctorily, since if it is not for the sake of sex that two strangers have penned themselves up together in such a cramped and comfortless living-space, then what reason have they for being there at all?

It all comes to a head when, while he is out of the flat, Jacqueline searches out his diary and reads what he has written about their life together. He returns to find her packing her belongings.

'What is going on?' he asks.

Tight-lipped, she points to the diary lying open on his desk.

He flares up in anger. 'You are not going to stop me from writing!' he vows. It is a non sequitur, and he knows it.

She is angry too, but in a colder, deeper way. 'If, *as you say*, you find me such an unspeakable burden,' she says, 'if I am destroying your peace and privacy and your ability to write, let

8

me tell you from my side that I have hated living with you, hated every minute of it, and can't wait to be free.'

What he should have said was that one should not read other people's private papers. In fact, he should have hidden his diary away, not left it where it could be found. But it is too late now, the damage is done.

He watches while Jacqueline packs, helps her strap her bag on the pillion of her scooter. 'I'll keep the key, *with your permission*, until I have fetched the rest of my stuff,' she says. She snaps on her helmet. 'Goodbye. I'm really disappointed in you, John. You may be very clever – I wouldn't know about that – but you have a lot of growing up to do.' She kicks the starter pedal. The engine will not catch. Again she kicks it, and again. A smell of petrol rises in the air. The carburettor is flooded; there is nothing to do but wait for it to dry out. 'Come inside,' he suggests. Stony-faced, she refuses. 'I'm sorry,' he says. 'About everything.'

He goes indoors, leaving her in the alley. Five minutes later he hears the engine start and the scooter roar off.

Is he sorry? Certainly he is sorry Jacqueline read what she read. But the real question is, what was his motive for writing what he wrote? Did he perhaps write it in order that she should read it? Was leaving his true thoughts lying around where she was bound to find them his way of telling her what he was too cowardly to say to her face? What are his true thoughts anyway? Some days he feels happy, even privileged, to be living with a beautiful woman, or at least not to be living alone. Other days he feels differently. Is the truth the happiness, the unhappiness, or the average of the two?

The question of what should be permitted to go into his diary and what kept forever shrouded goes to the heart of all his writing. If he is to censor himself from expressing ignoble emotions – resentment at having his flat invaded, or shame at

9

his own failures as a lover – how will those emotions ever be transfigured and turned into poetry? And if poetry is not to be the agency of his transfiguration from ignoble to noble, why bother with poetry at all? Besides, who is to say that the feelings he writes in his diary are his true feelings? Who is to say that at each moment while the pen moves he is truly himself? At one moment he might truly be himself, at another he might simply be making things up. How can he know for sure? Why should he even *want* to know for sure?

Things are rarely as they seem: that is what he should have said to Jacqueline. Yet what chance is there she would have understood? How could she believe that what she read in his diary was not the truth, the ignoble truth, about what was going on in the mind of her companion during those heavy evenings of silence and sighings but on the contrary a fiction, one of many possible fictions, true only in the sense that a work of art is true – true to itself, true to its own immanent aims – when the ignoble reading conformed so closely to her own suspicion that her companion did not love her, did not even like her?

Jacqueline will not believe him, for the simple reason that he does not believe himself. He does not know what he believes. Sometimes he thinks he does not believe anything. But when all is said and done, the fact remains that his first try at living with a woman has ended in failure, in ignominy. He must return to living by himself; and there will be no little relief in that. Yet he cannot live alone for ever. Having mistresses is part of an artist's life: even if he steers clear of the trap of marriage, as he will certainly do, he is going to have to find a way of living with women. Art cannot be fed on deprivation alone, on longing, loneliness. There must be intimacy, passion, love as well.

Picasso, who is a great artist, perhaps the greatest of all, is a living example. Picasso falls in love with women, one after another. One after another they move in with him, share his life, model for him. Out of the passion that flares up anew with each new mistress, the Doras and Pilars whom chance brings to his doorstep are reborn into everlasting art. That is how it is done. What of him? Can he promise that the women in his own life, not only Jacqueline but all the unimaginable women to come, will have a similar destiny? He would like to believe so, but he has his doubts. Whether he will turn out to be a great artist only time will tell, but one thing is sure, he is no Picasso. His whole sensibility is different from Picasso's. He is quieter, gloomier, more northern. Nor does he have Picasso's hypnotic black eyes. If ever he tries to transfigure a woman, he will not transfigure her as cruelly as Picasso does, bending and twisting her body like metal in a fiery furnace. Writers are not like painters anyway: they are more dogged, more subtle.

Is that the fate of all woman who become mixed up with artists: to have their worst or their best extracted and worked into fiction? He thinks of Hélène in *War and Peace*. Did Hélène start off as one of Tolstoy's mistresses? Did she ever guess that, long after she was gone, men who had never laid eyes on her would lust after her beautiful bare shoulders?

Must it all be so cruel? Surely there is a form of cohabitation in which man and woman eat together, sleep together, live together, yet remain immersed in their respective inward explorations. Is that why the affair with Jacqueline was doomed to fail: because, not being an artist herself, she could not appreciate the artist's need for inner solitude? If Jacqueline had been a sculptress, for instance, if one corner of the flat had been set aside for her to chip away at her marble while in another corner he wrestled with words and rhymes, would love have flourished between them? Is that the moral of the story of himself and Jacqueline: that it is best for artists to have affairs only with artists?

TWO

THE AFFAIR IS over. After weeks of smothering intimacy he has a room of his own again. He piles Jacqueline's boxes and suitcases in a corner and waits for them to be fetched. It does not happen. Instead, one evening, Jacqueline herself reappears. She has come, she says, not to resume residence with him ('You are impossible to live with') but to patch up a peace ('I don't like bad blood, it depresses me'), a peace that entails first going to bed with him, then, in bed, haranguing him about what he said about her in his diary. On and on she goes: they do not get to sleep until two in the morning.

He wakes up late, too late for his eight o'clock lecture. It is not the first lecture he has missed since Jacqueline entered his life. He is falling behind in his studies and does not see how he will ever catch up. In his first two years at the university he had been one of the stars of the class. He found everything easy, was always a step ahead of the lecturer. But of late a fog seems to have descended on his mind. The mathematics they are studying has become more modern and abstract, and he has begun to flounder. Line by line he can still follow the exposition on the blackboard, but more often than not the larger argument eludes him. He has fits of panic in class which he does his best to hide.

Strangely, he seems to be the only one afflicted. Even the plodders among his fellow students have no more trouble than usual. While his marks fall month by month, theirs remain steady. As for the stars, the real stars, they have simply left him struggling in their wake.

Never in his life has he had to call on his utmost powers. Less than his best has always been good enough. Now he is in a fight for his life. Unless he throws himself wholly into his work, he is going to sink.

Yet whole days pass in a fog of grey exhaustion. He curses himself for letting himself be sucked back into an affair that costs him so much. If this is what having a mistress entails, how do Picasso and the others get by? He simply has not the energy to run from lecture to lecture, job to job, then when the day is done to pay attention to a woman who veers between euphoria and spells of the blackest gloom in which she thrashes around brooding on a lifetime's grudges.

Although no longer formally living with him, Jacqueline feels free to arrive on his doorstep at all hours of the night and day. Sometimes she comes to denounce him for some word or other he let slip whose veiled meaning has only now become clear to her. Sometimes she is simply feeling low and wants to be cheered up. Worst is the day after therapy: she is there to rehearse, over and over again, what passed in her therapist's consulting room, to pick over the implications of his tiniest gesture. She sighs and weeps, gulps down glass after glass of wine, goes dead in the middle of sex.

'You should have therapy yourself,' she tells him, blowing smoke.

'I'll think about it,' he replies. He knows enough, by now, not to disagree.

In fact he would not dream of going into therapy. The goal

of therapy is to make one happy. What is the point of that? Happy people are not interesting. Better to accept the burden of unhappiness and try to turn it into something worthwhile, poetry or music or painting: that is what he believes.

Nevertheless, he listens to Jacqueline as patiently as he can. He is the man, she is the woman; he has had his pleasure of her, now he must pay the price: that seems to be the way affairs work.

Her story, spoken night after night in overlapping and conflicting versions into his sleep-befuddled ear, is that she has been robbed of her true self by a persecutor who is sometimes her tyrannical mother, sometimes her runaway father, sometimes one or other sadistic lover, sometimes a Mephistophelean therapist. What he holds in his arms, she says, is only a shell of her true self; she will recover the power to love only when she has recovered her self.

He listens but does not believe. If her therapist has designs on her, he thinks to himself, why doesn't she stop seeing him? If her sister disparages her, why not simply stop seeing her sister? As for himself, he suspects that if Jacqueline has come to treat him more as a confidant than as a lover, that is because he is not a good enough lover, not fiery enough, not passionate. He suspects that if he were more of a lover she would very soon find her missing self and her missing desire.

Why does he keep opening the door to her knock? It is because this is what artists do – stay up all night, get their lives into a tangle – or is it because, despite all, he is bemused by this sleek, undeniably handsome woman who feels no shame in wandering around the flat naked under his gaze?

Why is she so free in his presence? Is it to taunt him (for she can feel his eyes upon her, he knows that), or do all nurses behave like this in private, dropping their clothes, scratching themselves, talking matter-of-factly about excretion, telling the same gross jokes that men tell in bars? Yet if Jacqueline has freed herself of all inhibitions, why is her lovemaking so distracted, offhand, disappointing?

It was not his idea to begin the affair nor his idea to continue it. But now that he is in the middle of it he has not the energy to escape. A fatalism has taken him over. If life with Jacqueline is a kind of sickness, let the sickness take its course.

He and Paul are gentlemen enough not to compare notes on their mistresses. Nevertheless he suspects that Jacqueline Laurier discusses him with her sister and her sister reports back to Paul. It embarrasses him that Paul should know what goes on in his intimate life. He is sure that, of the two of them, Paul handles women more capably.

One evening when Jacqueline is working the night shift at the nursing home, he drops by at Paul's flat. He finds Paul preparing to set off for his mother's house in St James, to spend the weekend. Why does he not come along, suggests Paul, for the Saturday at least?

They miss the last train, by a hairsbreadth. If they still want to go to St James, they will have to walk the whole twelve miles. It is a fine evening. Why not?

Paul carries his rucksack and his violin. He is bringing the violin along, he says, because it is easier to practise in St James where the neighbours are not so close.

Paul has studied the violin since childhood but has never got very far with it. He seems quite content to play the same little gigues and minuets as a decade ago. His own ambitions as a musician are far larger. In his flat he has the piano that his mother bought when at the age of fifteen he began to demand piano lessons. The lessons were not a success, he was too impatient with the slow, step-by-step methods of his teacher. Nevertheless, he is determined that one day he will play, however badly, Beethoven's opus 132, and, after that, the Busoni transcription of Bach's D minor Chaconne. He will arrive at these goals without making the usual detour through Czerny and Mozart. Instead he will practise these two pieces and them alone, unremittingly, first learning the notes by playing them very, very slowly, then pushing up the tempo day by day, for as long as is required. It is his own method of learning the piano, invented by himself. As long as he follows his schedules without wavering he can see no reason why it should not work.

What he is finding, however, is that as he tries to progress from very, very slow to merely very slow, his wrists grow tense and lock, his finger-joints stiffen, and soon he cannot play at all. Then he flies into a rage, hammers his fists on the keys, and storms off in despair.

It is past midnight and he and Paul are no further than Wynberg. The traffic has died away, the Main Road is empty save for a street sweeper pushing his broom.

In Diep River they are passed by a milkman in his horse-drawn cart. They pause to watch as he reins in his horse, lopes up a garden path, sets down two full bottles, picks up the empties, shakes out the coins, lopes back to his cart.

'Can we buy a pint?' says Paul, and hands over fourpence. Smiling, the milkman watches while they drink. The milkman is young and handsome and bursting with energy. Even the big white horse with the shaggy hooves does not seem to mind being up in the middle of the night.

He marvels. All the business he knew nothing about, being carried on while people sleep: streets being swept, milk being delivered on doorsteps! But one thing puzzles him. Why is the milk not stolen? Why are there not thieves who follow in the milkman's footsteps and filch each bottle he sets down? In a land where property is crime and anything and everything can be stolen, what renders milk exempt? The fact that stealing it is too easy? Are there standards of conduct even among thieves? Or do thieves take pity on milkmen, who are for the most part young and black and powerless?

He would like to believe this last explanation. He would like to believe there is enough pity in the air for black people and their lot, enough of a desire to deal honourably with them, to make up for the cruelty of the laws. But he knows it is not so. Between black and white there is a gulf fixed. Deeper than pity, deeper than honourable dealings, deeper even than goodwill, lies an awareness on both sides that people like Paul and himself, with their pianos and violins, are here on this earth, the earth of South Africa, on the shakiest of pretexts. This very milkman, who a year ago must have been just a boy herding cattle in the deepest Transkei, must know it. In fact, from Africans in general, even from Coloured people, he feels a curious, amused tenderness emanating: a sense that he must be a simpleton, in need of protection, if he imagines he can get by on the basis of straight looks and honourable dealings when the ground beneath his feet is soaked with blood and the vast backward depth of history rings with shouts of anger. Why else would this young man, with the first stirrings of the day's wind fingering his horse's mane, smile so gently as he watches the two of them drink the milk he has given them?

They arrive at the house in St James as dawn is breaking. He falls asleep at once on a sofa, and sleeps until noon, when Paul's mother wakes them and serves breakfast on a sunporch with a view over the whole sweep of False Bay.

Between Paul and his mother there is a flow of conversation in which he is easily included. His mother is a photographer with a studio of her own. She is petite and well-dressed, with a smoker's husky voice and a restless air. After they have eaten she excuses herself: she has work to do, she says.

He and Paul walk down to the beach, swim, come back, play chess. Then he catches a train home. It is his first glimpse of Paul's home life, and he is full of envy. Why can he not have a nice, normal relationship with his own mother? He wishes his mother were like Paul's, wishes she had a life of her own outside their narrow family.

It was to escape the oppressiveness of family that he left home. Now he rarely sees his parents. Though they live only a short walk away, he does not visit. He has never brought Paul to see them, or any of his other friends, to say nothing of Jacqueline. Now that he has his own income, he uses his independence to exclude his parents from his life. His mother is distressed by his coldness, he knows, the coldness with which he has responded to her love all his life. All his life she has wanted to coddle him; all his life he has been resisting. Even though he insists, she cannot believe he has enough money to live on. Whenever she sees him she tries to slip money into his pocket, a pound note, two pounds. 'Just a little something,' she calls it. Given half a chance, she would sew curtains for his flat, take in his laundry. He must harden his heart against her. Now is not the time to let down his guard.

THREE

HE IS READING *The Letters of Ezra Pound*. Ezra Pound was dismissed from his job at Wabash College, Indiana, for having a woman in his rooms. Infuriated by such provincial smallmindedness, Pound quit America. In London he met and married the beautiful Dorothy Shakespear, and went to live in Italy. After World War II he was accused of aiding and abetting the Fascists. To escape the death sentence he pleaded insanity and was locked up in a mental asylum.

Now, in 1959, having been set free, Pound is back in Italy, still working on his life's project, the *Cantos*. All the *Cantos* that have been published thus far are in the University of Cape Town library, in Faber editions in which the procession of lines in elegant dark typeface is interrupted now and again, like strokes of a gong, by huge Chinese characters. He is engrossed by the *Cantos*; he reads and rereads them (guiltily skipping the dull sections on Van Buren and the Malatestas), using Hugh Kenner's book on Pound as a guide. T. S. Eliot magnanimously called Pound *il miglior fabbro*, the better craftsman. Much as he admires Eliot's own work, he thinks Eliot is right.

Ezra Pound has suffered persecution most of his life: driven into exile, then imprisoned, then expelled from his homeland a second time. Yet despite being labelled a madman Pound has proved he is a great poet, perhaps as great as Walt Whitman. Obeying his daimon, Pound has sacrificed his life to his art. So has Eliot, though Eliot's suffering has been of a more private nature. Eliot and Pound have lived lives of sorrow and sometimes of ignominy. There is a lesson for him in that, driven home on every page of their poetry – of Eliot's, with which he had his first overwhelming encounter while he was still at school, and now of Pound's. Like Pound and Eliot, he must be prepared to endure all that life has stored up for him, even if that means exile, obscure labour, and obloquy. And if he fails the highest test of art, if it turns out that after all he does not have the blessed gift, then he must be prepared to endure that too: the immovable verdict of history, the fate of being, despite all his present and future sufferings, minor. Many are called, few are chosen. For every major poet a cloud of minor poets, like gnats buzzing around a lion.

His passion for Pound is shared by only one of his friends, Norbert. Norbert was born in Czechoslovakia, came to South Africa after the War, and speaks English with a faint German lisp. He is studying to be an engineer, like his father. He dresses with elegant European formality and is conducting a highly respectable courtship of a beautiful girl of good family with whom he goes walking once a week. He and Norbert have meetings in a tea-room on the slopes of the mountain at which they comment on each other's latest poems and read aloud to each other favourite passages from Pound.

It strikes him as interesting that Norbert, an engineer to be, and he, a mathematician to be, should be disciples of Ezra Pound, while the other student poets he knows, those studying literature and running the university's literary magazine, follow Gerard Manley Hopkins. He himself went through a brief Hopkins phase at school, during which he crammed lots of stressed monosyllables into his verses and avoided words of Romance origin. But in time he lost his taste for Hopkins, just as he is in the process of losing his taste for Shakespeare. Hopkins's lines are packed too tight with consonants, Shakespeare's too tight with metaphors. Hopkins and Shakespeare also set too much store on uncommon words, particularly Old English words: *maw*, *reck*, *pelf*. He does not see why verse has always to be rising to a declamatory pitch, why it cannot be content to follow the flexions of the ordinary speaking voice – in fact, why it has to be so different from prose.

He has begun to prefer Pope to Shakespeare, and Swift to Pope. Despite the cruel precision of his phrasing, of which he approves, Pope strikes him as still too much at home among petticoats and periwigs, whereas Swift remains a wild man, a solitary.

He likes Chaucer too. The Middle Ages are boring, obsessed with chastity, overrun with clerics; medieval poets are for the most part timid, for ever scuttling to the Latin fathers for guidance. But Chaucer keeps a nice ironic distance from his authorities. And, unlike Shakespeare, he does not get into a froth about things and start ranting.

As for the other English poets, Pound has taught him to smell out the easy sentiment in which the Romantics and Victorians wallow, to say nothing of their slack versifying. Pound and Eliot are trying to revitalize Anglo-American poetry by bringing back to it the astringency of the French. He is fully in accord. How he could once have been so infatuated with Keats as to write Keatsian sonnets he cannot comprehend. Keats is like watermelon, soft and sweet and crimson, whereas poetry should be hard and clear like a flame. Reading half a dozen pages of Keats is like yielding to seduction.

He would be more secure in his discipleship to Pound if he could actually read French. But all his efforts to teach himself lead nowhere. He has no feel for the language, with its words that start out boldly only to tail off in a murmur. So he must take it on trust from Pound and Eliot that Baudelaire and Nerval, Corbière and Laforgue, point the way he must follow.

His plan, when he entered the university, was to qualify as a mathematician, then go abroad and devote himself to art. That is as far as the plan went, as far as it needed to go, and he has not thus far deviated from it. While perfecting his poetic skills abroad he will earn a living doing something obscure and respectable. Since great artists are fated to go unrecognized for a while, he imagines he will serve out his probationary years as a clerk humbly adding up columns of figures in a back room. He will certainly not be a Bohemian, that is to say, a drunk and a sponger and a layabout.

What draws him to mathematics, besides the arcane symbols it uses, is its purity. If there were a department of Pure Thought at the university he would probably enrol in pure thought too; but pure mathematics appears to be the closest approach the academy affords to the realm of the forms.

There is one obstacle to his plan of study, however: regulations do not permit one to study pure mathematics to the exclusion of everything else. Most of the students in his class do a mix of pure mathematics, applied mathematics, and physics. This is not a direction he finds himself able to follow. Though as a child he had a desultory interest in rocketry and nuclear fission, he has no feel for what is called the real world, fails to understand why things in physics are as they are. Why, for instance, does a bouncing ball eventually stop bouncing? His fellow students have no difficulty with the question: because its coefficient of elasticity is less than one, they say. But why does it have to be so, he asks?

Why can the coefficient not be exactly one, or more than one? They shrug their shoulders. We live in the real world, they say: in the real world the coefficient of elasticity is always less than one. It does not sound to him like an answer.

Since he would appear to have no sympathy with the real world, he avoids the sciences, filling in the empty slots in his curriculum with courses in English, philosophy, classical studies. He would like to be thought of as a mathematics student who happens to take a few arts courses; but among the science students he is, to his chagrin, viewed as an outsider, a dilettante who turns up for mathematics lectures and then disappears, God knows where.

Since he is going to be a mathematician, he ought to spend most of his time on mathematics. But mathematics is easy, whereas Latin is not. Latin is his weakest subject. Years of drilling at his Catholic school have embedded in him the logic of Latin syntax; he can write correct if plodding Ciceronian prose; but Virgil and Horace, with their haphazard word order and rebarbative word-stock, continue to baffle him.

He is assigned to a Latin tutorial group in which most of the other students take Greek as well. Knowing Greek makes Latin easy for them; he has to struggle to keep up, not to make a fool of himself. He wishes he had gone to a school that taught Greek.

One of the secret attractions of mathematics is that it uses the Greek alphabet. Though he knows no Greek words beyond *hubris* and *arete* and *eleutheria*, he spends hours perfecting his Greek script, pressing harder on the down-strokes to give the effect of a Bodoni typeface.

Greek and pure mathematics are in his eyes the noblest subjects one can study at a university. From afar he reveres the lecturers in Greek, whose courses he cannot take: Anton Paap, papyrologist; Maurice Pope, translator of Sophocles; Maurits Heemstra,

23

commentator on Heraclitus. Together with Douglas Sears, Professor of Pure Mathematics, they inhabit an exalted realm.

Despite his best efforts, his marks for Latin are not high. It is Roman history that brings him down every time. The lecturer assigned to teach Roman history is a pale, unhappy young Englishman whose real interest is *Digenis Akritas*. The law students, taking Latin under compulsion, sense his weakness and torment him. They come in late and leave early; they throw paper aeroplanes; they whisper loudly while he is talking; when he produces one of his limp witticisms they laugh raucously and drum with their feet and will not stop.

The truth is, he is as bored as the law students, and perhaps their lecturer too, by fluctuations in the price of wheat during the reign of Commodus. Without facts there is no history, and he has never had a head for facts: when examinations come around and he is invited to offer his thoughts on what caused what in the late Empire, he stares at the empty page in misery.

They read Tacitus in translation: dry recitals of the excesses and outrages of the emperors in which only the inexplicable hurry of sentence after sentence hints at irony. If he is going to be a poet he ought to be taking lessons from Catullus, poet of love, whom they are translating in tutorials; but it is Tacitus the historian, whose Latin is so difficult that he cannot follow it in the original, who truly grips him.

Following Pound's recommendation, he has read Flaubert, first *Madame Bovary*, then *Salammbô*, Flaubert's novel of ancient Carthage, just as he has sternly refrained from reading Victor Hugo. Hugo is a windbag, says Pound, whereas Flaubert brings to the writing of prose the hard, jeweller's craft of poetry. Out of Flaubert come first Henry James, then Conrad and Ford Madox Ford.

He likes Flaubert. Emma Bovary in particular, with her dark

eyes, her restless sensuality, her readiness to give herself, has him in her thrall. He would like to go to bed with Emma, hear the famous belt whistle like a snake as she undresses. But would Pound approve? He is not sure that wanting to meet Emma is a good enough reason for admiring Flaubert. In his sensibility there is still, he suspects, something rotten, something Keatsian.

Of course Emma Bovary is a fictional creation, he will never run into her in the street. But Emma was not created out of nothing: she had her origin in the flesh and blood experiences of her author, experiences that were then subjected to the transfiguring fire of art. If Emma had an original, or several originals, then it follows that women like Emma and Emma's original should exist in the real world. And even if this is not so, even if no woman in the real world is quite like Emma, there must be many women so deeply affected by their reading of *Madame Bovary* that they fall under Emma's spell and are transformed into versions of her. They may not be the real Emma but in a sense they are her living embodiment.

His ambition is to read everything worth reading before he goes overseas, so that he will not arrive in Europe a provincial bumpkin. As guides to reading he relies upon Eliot and Pound. On their authority he dismisses without a glance shelf after shelf of Scott, Dickens, Thackeray, Trollope, Meredith. Nor is anything that came out of nineteenth-century Germany or Italy or Spain or Scandinavia worthy of attention. Russia may have produced some interesting monsters but as artists the Russians have nothing to teach. Civilization since the eighteenth century has been an Anglo-French affair.

On the other hand, there are pockets of high civilization in remoter times that one cannot afford to neglect: not only Athens and Rome but also the Germany of Walther von der Vogelweide, the Provence of Arnaut Daniel, the Florence of Dante and Guido

Cavalcanti, to say nothing of Tang China and Moghul India and Almoravid Spain. So unless he learns Chinese and Persian and Arabic, or at least enough of the languages to read their classics with a crib, he might as well be a barbarian. Where will he find the time?

In his English courses he did not at the beginning fare well. His tutor in literature was a young Welshman named Mr Jones. Mr Jones was new to South Africa; this was his first proper job. The law students, enrolled only because English, like Latin, was a required subject, had sniffed out his uncertainty at once: they yawned in his face, played stupid, parodied his speech, until sometimes he grew quite desperate.

Their first assignment was to write a critical analysis of a poem by Andrew Marvell. Though not sure what exactly was meant by critical analysis, he did his best. Mr Jones gave him a gamma. Gamma was not the lowest mark on the scale – there was still gamma-minus, to say nothing of the varieties of delta – but it was not good. Numbers of students, including law students, were awarded betas; there was even a solitary alpha-minus. Indifferent to poetry though they might be, there was something these classmates of his knew that he did not. But what was it? How did one get to be good at English?

Mr Jones, Mr Bryant, Miss Wilkinson: all his teachers were young and, it seemed to him, helpless, suffering the persecutions of the law students in silence, hoping they would grow tired and relent. As for himself, he felt little sympathy for their plight. What he wanted from his teachers was authority, not an exhibition of vulnerability.

In the three years since Mr Jones, his marks for English have slowly crept up. But he has never been at the top of the class, has always, in a certain sense, been struggling, unsure of what

the study of literature ought to be. Compared with literary criticism, the philological side of English has been a relief. At least
with Old English verb conjugations or sound changes in Middle
English one knows where one is.

Now, in his fourth year, he has enrolled for a course in early
English prose writers taught by Professor Guy Howarth. He is
the only student. Howarth has a reputation for being dry, pedan-
tic, but he does not mind that. He has nothing against pedants.
He prefers them to showmen.

They meet once a week in Howarth's office. Howarth reads
his lecture aloud while he takes notes. After a few meetings
Howarth simply lends him the text of the lecture to take home
and read.

The lectures, which are typed in faint ribbon on crisp,
yellowing paper, come out of a cabinet in which there seems
to be a file on every English-language author from Austen to
Yeats. Is that what one has to do to become a professor of
English: read the established authors and write a lecture on
each? How many years of one's life does that eat up? What
does it do to one's spirit?

Howarth, who is an Australian, seems to have taken a liking
to him, he cannot see why. For his part, though he cannot say
he likes Howarth, he does feel protective of him for his gaucherie,
for his delusion that South African students care in the least
what he thinks about Gascoigne or Lyly or for that matter
Shakespeare.

On the last day of term, after their final session together,
Howarth issues an invitation. 'Come by the house tomorrow
evening for a drink.'

He obeys, but with a sinking heart. Beyond their exchanges
on the Elizabethan prosaists, he has nothing to say to Howarth.
In addition, he does not like drinking. Even wine, after the first

sip, tastes sour to him, sour and heavy and unpleasant. He cannot see why people pretend to enjoy it.

They sit in the dim, high-ceilinged living room of the Howarths' home in the Gardens. He appears to be the only one invited. Howarth talks about Australian poetry, about Kenneth Slessor and A. D. Hope. Mrs Howarth breezes in, breezes out again. He senses that she does not like him, finds him a prig, lacking in *joie de vivre*, lacking in repartee. Lilian Howarth is Howarth's second wife. No doubt she was a beauty in her day, but now she is simply a squat little woman with spindly legs and too much powder on her face. She is also, according to report, a lush, given to embarrassing scenes when drunk.

It emerges that he has been invited for a purpose. The Howarths are going abroad for six months. Would he be prepared to stay in their house and look after it? There will be no rent to pay, no bills, few responsibilities.

He accepts on the spot. He is flattered to be asked, even if it is only because he seems dull and dependable. Also, if he gives up his flat in Mowbray, he can save more quickly toward a boat ticket to England. And the house – a huge, rambling pile on the lower slopes of the mountain with dark passages and musty, unused rooms – has an allure of its own.

There is one catch. For the first month he will have to share the house with guests of the Howarths, a woman from New Zealand and her three-year-old daughter.

The woman from New Zealand turns out to be another drinker. Shortly after he has moved in, she wanders into his room in the middle of the night and into his bed. She embraces him, presses against him, gives him wet kisses. He does not know what to do. He does not like her, does not desire her, is repelled by her slack lips seeking out his mouth. First a cold shiver runs

28

through him, then panic. 'No!' he cries out. 'Go away!' And he curls himself up in a ball.

Unsteadily she clambers out of his bed. 'Bastard!' she hisses, and is gone.

They continue to share the big house until the end of the month, avoiding each other, listening for the creak of a floorboard, averting their gaze when their paths happen to cross. They have made fools of themselves, but at least she was a reckless fool, which is forgivable, while he was a prude and a dummy.

He has never been drunk in his life. He abhors drunkenness. He leaves parties early to escape the stumbling, inane talk of people who have drunk too much. In his opinion, drunken drivers ought to have their sentences doubled instead of halved. But in South Africa every excess committed under the influence of liquor is looked on indulgently. Farmers can flog their labourers to death as long as they are drunk when they do so. Ugly men can force themselves on women, ugly women make overtures to men; if one resists, one is not playing the game.

He has read Henry Miller. If a drunken woman had slipped into bed with Henry Miller, the fucking and no doubt the drinking as well would have gone on all night. Were Henry Miller merely a satyr, a monster of indiscriminate appetite, he could be ignored. But Henry Miller is an artist, and his stories, outrageous though they may be and probably full of lies, are stories of an artist's life. Henry Miller writes about the Paris of the 1930s, a city of artists and women who loved artists. If women threw themselves at Henry Miller, then, *mutatis mutandis*, they must have thrown themselves at Ezra Pound and Ford Madox Ford and Ernest Hemingway and all the other great artists who lived in Paris in those years, to say nothing of Pablo Picasso. What is *he* going to do once he is in Paris or London? Is he going to persist in not playing the game?

Besides his horror of drunkenness he has a horror of physical ugliness. When he reads Villon's *Testament*, he can think only of how ugly the *belle heaumière* sounds, wrinkled and unwashed and foulmouthed. If one is to be an artist, must one love women indiscriminately? Does an artist's life entail sleeping with anyone and everyone, in the name of life? If one is finicky about sex, is one rejecting life?

Another question: What made Marie, from New Zealand, decide he was worth getting into bed with? Was it simply because he was there, or had she heard from Howarth that he was a poet, a poet to be? Women love artists because they burn with an inner flame, a flame that consumes yet paradoxically renews all that it touches. When she slipped into his bed, Marie must have thought she would be licked by the flame of art, and experience an ecstasy beyond words. Instead she found herself being pushed away by a panic-stricken boy. Surely, one way or another, she will have her revenge. Surely, in the next letter from her, her friends the Howarths will get a version of events in which he will come out looking like a nincompoop.

He knows that to condemn a woman for being ugly is morally despicable. But fortunately, artists do not have to be morally admirable people. All that matters is that they create great art. If his own art is to come out of the more contemptible side of himself, so be it. Flowers grow best on dungheaps, as Shakespeare never tires of saying. Even Henry Miller, who presents himself as such a straightforward fellow, ready to make love to any woman no matter her shape or size, probably has a dark side which he is prudent enough to conceal.

Normal people find it hard to be bad. Normal people, when they feel badness flare up within them, drink, swear, commit violence. Badness is to them like a fever: they want it out of their system, they want to go back to being normal. But artists have to live with their fever, whatever its nature, good or bad. The fever is what makes them artists; the fever must be kept alive. That is why artists can never be wholly present to the world: one eye has always to be turned inward. As for women who flock after artists, they cannot wholly be trusted. For just as the spirit of the artist is both flame and fever, so the woman who yearns to be licked by tongues of flame will at the same time do her best to quench the fever and bring down the artist to common ground. Therefore women have to be resisted even when they are loved. They cannot be allowed close enough to the flame to nip it out.

FOUR

IN A PERFECT world he would sleep only with perfect women, women of perfect femininity yet with a certain darkness at their core that will respond to his own darker self. But he knows no such women. Jacqueline – any darkness at whose core he has failed to detect – has without warning ceased visiting him, and he has had the good sense not to try to find out why. So he has to make do with other women – in fact with girls who are not yet women and may have no authentic core at all, or none to speak of: girls who sleep with a man only reluctantly, because they have been talked into it or because their friends are doing it and they don't want to be left behind or because it is sometimes the only way to hold on to a boyfriend.

He gets one of them pregnant. When she telephones to break the news, he is astonished, floored. How could he have got someone pregnant? In a certain sense he knows exactly how. An accident: haste, confusion, a mess of the kind that never finds its way into the novels he reads. Yet at the same time he cannot believe it. In his heart he does not feel himself to be more than eight years old, ten at the most. How can a child be a father?

Perhaps it is not true, he tells himself. Perhaps it is like one of those exams you are sure you have failed, yet when the results come out you have not done badly after all.

But it does not work like that. Another telephone call. In matter-of-fact tones the girl reports that she has seen a doctor. There is the tiniest pause, long enough for him to accept the opening and speak. 'I will stand by you,' he could say. 'Leave it all to me,' he could say. But how can he say he will stand by her when what *standing by her* will mean in reality fills him with foreboding, when his whole impulse is to drop the telephone and run away?

The pause comes to an end. She has the name, she continues, of someone who will take care of the problem. She has accordingly made an appointment for the next day. Is he prepared to drive her to the place of appointment and bring her back afterwards, since she has been advised that after the event she will be in no state to drive?

Her name is Sarah. Her friends call her Sally, a name he does not like. It reminds him of the line 'Come down to the sally gardens.' What on earth are sally gardens? She comes from Johannesburg, from one of those suburbs where people spend their Sundays cantering around the estate on horseback calling out 'Jolly good!' to each other while black menservants wearing white gloves bring them drinks. A childhood of cantering around on horses and falling off and hurting herself but not crying has turned Sarah into a brick. 'Sal is a real brick,' he can hear her Johannesburg set saying. She is not beautiful – too solid-boned, too fresh-faced for that – but she is healthy through and through. And she does not pretend. Now that disaster has struck, she does not hide away in her room pretending nothing is wrong. On the contrary, she has found out what needs to be found out – how to get an abortion in Cape Town – and has made the necessary arrangements. In fact, she has put him to shame.

In her little car they drive to Woodstock and stop before a

33

row of identical little semi-detached houses. She gets out and knocks at the door of one of them. He does not see who opens it, but it can be no one but the abortionist herself. He imagines abortionists as blowsy women with dyed hair and caked makeup and none too clean fingernails. They give the girl a glass of neat gin, make her lie back, then carry out some unspeakable manipulation inside her with a piece of wire, something that involves hooking and dragging. Sitting in the car, he shudders. Who would guess that in an ordinary house like this, with hydrangeas in the garden and a plaster gnome, such horrors go on!

Half an hour passes. He grows more and more nervous. Is he going to be able to do what will be required of him?

Then Sarah emerges, and the door closes behind her. Slowly, with an air of concentration, she walks toward the car. When she gets closer he sees she is pale and sweating. She does not speak.

He drives her to the Howarths' big house and instals her in the bedroom overlooking Table Bay and the harbour. He offers her tea, offers her soup, but she wants nothing. She has brought a suitcase; she has brought her own towels, her own sheets. She has thought of everything. He has merely to be around, be ready if something goes wrong. It is not much to expect.

She asks for a warm towel. He puts a towel in the electric oven. It comes out smelling of burn. By the time he has brought it upstairs it can barely be called warm. But she lays it on her belly and closes her eyes and seems to be soothed by it.

Every few hours she takes one of the pills the woman has given her, followed by water, glass after glass. For the rest she lies with her eyes closed, enduring the pain. Sensing his squeamishness, she has hidden from his sight the evidence of what is going on inside her body: the bloody pads and whatever else there is.

'How are you?' he asks.

'Fine,' she murmurs.

What he will do if she ceases to be fine, he has no idea. Abortion is illegal, but how illegal? If he called in a doctor, would the doctor report them to the police?

He sleeps on a mattress at the bedside. As a nurse he is useless, worse than useless. What he is doing cannot in fact be called nursing. It is merely a penance, a stupid and ineffectual penance.

On the morning of the third day she appears at the door of the study downstairs, pale and swaying on her feet but fully dressed. She is ready to go home, she says.

He drives her to her lodgings, with her suitcase and the laundry bag that presumably contains the bloody towels and sheets. 'Would you like me to stay a while?' he asks. She shakes her head. 'I'll be all right,' she says. He kisses her on the cheek and walks home.

She has issued no reproofs, made no demands; she has even paid the abortionist herself. In fact, she has taught him a lesson in how to behave. As for him, he has emerged ignominiously, he cannot deny it. What help he has given her has been faint-hearted and, worse, incompetent. He prays she will never tell the story to anyone.

His thoughts keep going to what was destroyed inside her – that pod of flesh, that rubbery manikin. He sees the little creature flushed down the toilet at the Woodstock house, tumbled through the maze of sewers, tossed out at last into the shallows, blinking in the sudden sun, struggling against the waves that will carry it out into the bay. He did not want it to live and now he does not want it to die. Yet even if he were to run down to the beach, find it, save it from the sea, what would he do with it? Bring it home, keep it warm in cotton wool, try to get it to grow? How can he who is still a child bring up a child?

He is out of his depth. He has barely emerged into the world himself and already he has a death chalked up against him. How many of the other men he sees in the streets carry dead children with them like baby-shoes slung around their necks?

He would rather not see Sarah again. If he could be by himself he might be able to recover, return to being as he used to be. But to desert her now would be too shameful. So each day he drops by at her room and sits holding her hand for a decent period. If he has nothing to say, it is because he has not the courage to ask what is happening to her, in her. Is it like a sickness, he wonders to himself, from which she is now in the process of recuperating, or is it like an amputation, from which one never recovers? What is the difference between an abortion and a miscarriage and what in books is called *losing a child*? In books a woman who loses a child shuts herself off from the world and goes into mourning. Is Sarah still due to enter a time of mourning? And what of him? Is he too going to mourn? How long does one mourn, if one mourns? Does the mourning come to an end, and is one the same after the mourning as before; or does one mourn forever for the little thing that bobs in the waves off Woodstock, like the little cabin-boy who fell overboard and was not missed? *Weep, weep!* cries the cabin-boy, who will not sink and will not be stilled.

To bring in more money, he takes on a second afternoon of tutoring in the Mathematics Department. The first-year students who attend the tutorial are free to bring in questions on applied mathematics as well as pure mathematics. With only a single year of applied mathematics to his credit, he is barely ahead of the students he is supposed to be assisting: each week he has to spend hours on preparation.

Wrapped up though he is in his private worries, he cannot

fail to see that the country around him is in turmoil. The pass laws to which Africans and Africans alone are subjected are being tightened even further, and protests are breaking out everywhere. In the Transvaal the police fire shots into a crowd, then, in their mad way, go on firing into the backs of fleeing men, women and children. From beginning to end the business sickens him: the laws themselves; the bully-boy police; the government, stridently defending the murderers and denouncing the dead; and the press, too frightened to come out and say what anyone with eyes in his head can see.

After the carnage of Sharpeville nothing is as it was before. Even in the pacific Cape there are strikes and marches. Wherever a march takes place there are policemen with guns hovering around the edges, waiting for an excuse to shoot.

It all comes to a head one afternoon while he is on tutorial duty. The tutorial room is quiet; he is patrolling from desk to desk, checking how students are getting on with the assigned exercises, trying to help those in difficulty. Suddenly the door swings open. One of the senior lecturers strides in and raps on the table. 'May I have your attention!' he calls out. There is a nervous crack in his voice; his face is flushed. 'Please put down your pens and give me your attention! There is at this moment a workers' march taking place along De Waal Drive. For reasons of safety, I am asked to announce that no one is being allowed to leave the campus, until further notice. I repeat: no one is being allowed to leave. This is an order issued by the police. Are there any questions?'

There is one question at least, but this is not the right time to voice it: What is the country coming to when one cannot run a mathematics tutorial in peace? As for the police order, he does not believe for a moment that the police are sealing off the campus for the sake of the students. They are sealing it off

37

so that students from this notorious hotbed of leftism will not join the march, that is all.

There is no hope of continuing with the mathematics tutorial. Around the room there is a buzz of conversation; students are already packing their bags and exiting, eager to see what is up.

He follows the crowd to the embankment above De Waal Drive. All traffic has been halted. The marchers are coming up Woolsack Road in a thick snake, ten, twenty abreast, then turning north on to the motorway. They are men, most of them, in drab clothing – overalls, army surplus coats, woollen caps – some carrying sticks, all walking swiftly, silently. There is no end to the column in sight. If he were the police, he would be frightened.

'It's PAC,' says a Coloured student nearby. His eyes glisten, he has an intent look. Is he right? How does he know? Are there signs one ought to recognize? The PAC is not like the ANC. It is more ominous. *Africa for the Africans!* says the PAC. *Drive the whites into the sea!*

Thousands upon thousands, the column of men winds its way up the hill. It does not look like an army, but that is what it is, an army called into being of a sudden out of the wastelands of the Cape Flats. Once they reach the city, what will they do? Whatever it is, there are not enough policemen in the land to stop them, not enough bullets to kill them.

When he was twelve he was herded into a bus full of schoolchildren and driven to Adderley Street, where they were given paper orange-white-and-blue flags and told to wave them as the parade of floats passed by (Jan van Riebeeck and his wife in sober burgher dress; Voortrekkers with muskets; portly Paul Kruger). Three hundred years of history, three hundred years of Christian civilization at the tip of Africa, said the politicians in their speeches: to the Lord let us give thanks. Now, before his eyes, the Lord is withdrawing his protective hand. In the shadow of the mountain he is watching history being unmade.

In the hush around him, among these neat, well-dressed products of Rondebosch Boys High School and the Diocesan College, these youths who half an hour ago were busy calculating angles of vector and dreaming of careers as civil engineers, he can feel the same shock of dismay. They were expecting to enjoy a show, to snicker at a procession of garden boys, not to behold this grim host. The afternoon is ruined for them; all they want now is to go home, have a Coke and a sandwich, forget what has passed.

And he? He is no different. *Will the ships still be sailing tomorrow?* – that is his one thought. *I must get out before it is too late!*

The next day, when it is all over and the marchers have gone home, the newspapers find ways of talking about it. *Giving vent to pent-up anger,* they call it. *One of many protest marches countrywide in the wake of Sharpeville. Defused,* they say, *by the good sense (for once) of the police and the co-operation of march leaders. The government,* they say, *would be well advised to sit up and take note.* So they tame the event, making it less than what it was. He is not deceived. The merest whistle, and from the shacks and barracks of the Cape Flats the same army of men will spring up, stronger than before, more numerous. Armed too, with guns from China. What hope is there of standing against them when you do not believe in what you are standing for?

There is the matter of the Defence Force. When he left school they were conscripting only one white boy in three for military training. He was lucky enough not to be balloted. Now all that is changing. There are new rules. At any time he can find a call-up notice in his letterbox: *You are required to present yourself at the Castle at 9 a.m. on such-and-such a date. Bring only toilet items.*

Voortrekkerhoogte, somewhere in the Transvaal, is the training camp he has heard the most about. It is where they send conscripts from the Cape, far from home, to break them. In a week he could find himself behind barbed wire in Voortrekkerhoogte, sharing a tent with thuggish Afrikaners, eating bully-beef out of cans, listening to Johnnie Ray on Springbok Radio. He would not be able to endure it; he would slash his wrists. There is only one course open: to flee. But how can he flee without taking his degree? It would be like departing on a long journey, a life's journey, with no clothes, no money, no (the comparison comes more reluctantly) weapon.

FIVE

IT IS LATE, past midnight. In the faded blue sleeping-bag he has brought from South Africa, he is lying on the sofa in his friend Paul's bedsitter in Belsize Park. On the other side of the room, in the proper bed, Paul has begun to snore. Through a gap in the curtain glares a night sky of sodium orange tinged with violet. Though he has covered his feet with a cushion, they remain icy. No matter: he is in London.

There are two, perhaps three places in the world where life can be lived at its fullest intensity: London, Paris, perhaps Vienna. Paris comes first: city of love, city of art. But to live in Paris one must have gone to the kind of upper-class school that teaches French. As for Vienna, Vienna is for Jews coming back to reclaim their birthright: logical positivism, twelve-tone music, psychoanalysis. That leaves London, where South Africans do not need to carry papers and where people speak English. London may be stony, labyrinthine, and cold, but behind its forbidding walls men and women are at work writing books, painting paintings, composing music. One passes them every day in the street without guessing their secret, because of the famous and admirable British reserve.

For a half-share of the bedsitter, which consists of a single room and an annex with a gas stove and cold-water sink (the bathroom and toilet upstairs serve the whole house), he pays

Paul two pounds a week. His entire savings, which he has brought with him from South Africa, amount to eighty-four pounds. He must find a job at once.

He visits the offices of the London County Council and enters his name on a list of relief teachers, teachers ready to fill vacancies at short notice. He is sent for an interview to a secondary modern school in Barnet at the far end of the Northern Line. His degree is in mathematics and English. The headmaster wants him to teach social studies; in addition, to supervise swimming two afternoons a week.

'But I can't swim,' he objects.

'Then you'll have to learn, won't you?' says the headmaster.

He leaves the school premises with a copy of the social studies textbook under his arm. He has the weekend to prepare for his first class. By the time he gets to the station he is cursing himself for accepting the job. But he is too much of a coward to go back and say he has changed his mind. From the post office in Belsize Park he mails the book back, with a note: 'Unforeseen eventualities make it impossible for me to take up my duties. Please accept my sincerest apologies.'

An advertisement in the *Guardian* takes him on a trip to Rothamsted, the agricultural station outside London where Halsted and MacIntyre, authors of *The Design of Statistical Experiments*, one of his university textbooks, used to work. The interview, preceded by a tour of the station's gardens and greenhouses, goes well. The post he has applied for is that of Junior Experimental Officer. The duties of a JEO, he learns, consist in laying out grids for test plantings, recording yields under different regimens, then analyzing the data on the station's computer, all under the direction of one of the Senior Officers. The actual agricultural work is done by gardeners supervised by Agricultural Officers; he will not be expected to get his hands dirty.

A few days later a letter arrives confirming that he is being offered the job, at a salary of six hundred pounds a year. He cannot contain his joy. What a coup! To work at Rothamsted! People in South Africa will not believe it!

There is one catch. The letter ends: 'Accommodation can be arranged in the village or on the council housing estate.' He writes back: he accepts the offer, he says, but would prefer to go on living in London. He will commute to Rothamsted.

In reply he receives a telephone call from the personnel office. Commuting will not be practicable, he is told. What he is being offered is not a desk job with regular hours. On some mornings he will have to start work very early; at other times he will have to work late, or over weekends. Like all officers, he will therefore have to reside within reach of the station. Will he reconsider his position and communicate a final decision?

His triumph is dashed. What is the point of coming all the way from Cape Town to London if he is to be quartered on a housing estate miles outside the city, getting up at the crack of dawn to measure the height of bean plants? He wants to join Rothamsted, wants to find a use for the mathematics he has laboured over for years, but he also wants to go to poetry readings, meet writers and painters, have love affairs. How can he ever make the people at Rothamsted – men in tweed jackets smoking pipes, women with stringy hair and owlish glasses – understand that? How can he bring out words like *love*, *poetry* before them?

Yet how can he turn the offer down? He is within inches of having a real job, and in England too. He need only say one word – *Yes* – and he will be able to write to his mother giving her the news she is waiting to hear, namely that her son is earning a good salary doing something respectable. Then she in turn will be able to telephone his father's sisters and announce, 'John is working as a scientist in England.' *That* will finally put an end to their carping and sneering. A scientist: what could be more solid than that?

Solidity is what he has always lacked. Solidity is his Achilles' heel. Of cleverness he has enough (though not as much as his mother thinks, and as he himself once thought); solid he has never been. Rothamsted would give him, if not solidity, not at once, then at least a title, an office, a shell. Junior Experimental Officer, then one day Experimental Officer, Senior Experimental Officer: surely behind so eminently respectable a shield, in private, in secrecy, he will be able to go on with the work of transmuting experience into art, the work for which he was brought into the world.

That is the argument for the agricultural station. The argument against the agricultural station is that it is not in London, city of romance.

He writes to Rothamsted. On mature reflection, he says, taking into consideration all circumstances, he thinks it best to decline.

The newspapers are full of advertisements for computer programmers. A degree in science is recommended but not required. He has heard of computer programming but has no clear idea of what it is. He has never laid eyes on a computer, except in cartoons, where computers appear as box-like objects spitting out scrolls of paper. There are no computers in South Africa that he knows of.

He responds to the advertisement by IBM, IBM being the biggest and best, and goes for an interview wearing the black suit he bought before he left Cape Town. The IBM interviewer, a man in his thirties, wears a black suit of his own, but of smarter, leaner cut.

The first thing the interviewer wants to know is whether he has left South Africa for good.

He has, he replies.

Why, asks the interviewer?

'Because the country is heading for revolution,' he replies.

There is a silence. *Revolution*: not the right word, perhaps, for the halls of IBM.

'And when would you say,' says the interviewer, 'that this revolution will take place?'

He has his answer ready. 'Five years.' That is what everyone has said since Sharpeville. Sharpeville signalled the beginning of the end for the white régime, the *increasingly desperate* white régime.

After the interview he is given an IQ test. He has always enjoyed IQ tests, always done well at them. Generally he is better at tests, quizzes, examinations than at real life.

Within days IBM offers him a position as a trainee programmer. If he does well in his training course, and then passes his probationary period, he will become first a Programmer proper, then one day a Senior Programmer. He will commence his career at IBM's data-processing bureau in Newman Street, off Oxford Street in the heart of the West End. The hours will be nine to five. His initial salary will be seven hundred pounds a year.

He accepts the terms without hesitation.

The same day he passes a placard in the London Underground, a job advertisement. Applications are invited for the position of trainee station foreman, at a salary of seven hundred pounds a year. Minimum educational requirement: a school certificate. Minimum age: twenty-one.

Are all jobs in England paid equally, he wonders? If so, what is the point of having a degree?

In his programming course he finds himself in the company of two other trainees – a rather attractive girl from New Zealand

and a young Londoner with a spotty face – and a dozen or so IBM clients, businessmen. By rights he ought to be the best of the lot, he and perhaps the girl from New Zealand, who also has a mathematics degree; but in fact he struggles to understand what is going on and does badly in the written exercises. At the end of the first week they write a test, which he barely scrapes through. The instructor is not pleased with him and does not hesitate to express his displeasure. He is in the world of business, and in the world of business, he discovers, one does not need to be polite.

There is something about programming that flummoxes him, yet that even the businessmen in the class have no trouble with. In his naïveté he had imagined that computer programming would be about ways of translating symbolic logic and set theory into digital codes. Instead the talk is all about inventories and outflows, about Customer A and Customer B. What are inventories and outflows, and what have they to do with mathematics? He might as well be a clerk sorting cards into batches; he might as well be a trainee station foreman.

At the end of the third week he writes his final test, passes in undistinguished fashion, and graduates to Newman Street, where he is allocated a desk in a room with nine other young programmers. All the office furniture is grey. In the desk drawer he finds paper, a ruler, pencils, a pencil sharpener, and a little appointments book with a black plastic cover. On the cover, in solid capitals, is the word THINK. On the supervisor's desk, in his cubicle off the main office, is a sign reading THINK. THINK is the motto of IBM. What is special about IBM, he is given to understand, is that it is unrelentingly committed to thinking. It is up to employees to think at all times, and thus to live up to the ideal of IBM's founder Thomas J. Watson. Employees who do not think do not belong in IBM, which is the aristocrat of the business machine world. At its headquarters in White Plains,

New York, IBM has laboratories in which more cutting-edge research in computer science is performed than in all the universities of the world together. Scientists in White Plains are paid better than university professors, and provided with everything they can conceivably need. All they are required to do in return is think.

Though the hours at the Newman Street bureau are nine to five, he soon discovers that it is frowned upon for male employees to leave the premises promptly at five. Female employees with families to take care of may leave at five without reproach; men are expected to work until at least six. When there is a rush job they may have to work all night, with a break to go to a pub for a bite. Since he dislikes pubs, he simply works straight through. He rarely gets home before ten o'clock.

He is in England, in London; he has a job, a proper job, better than mere teaching, for which he is being paid a salary. He has escaped South Africa. Everything is going well, he has attained his first goal, he ought to be happy. In fact, as the weeks pass, he finds himself more and more miserable. He has attacks of panic, which he beats off with difficulty. In the office there is nothing to rest the eye on but flat metallic surfaces. Under the shadowless glare of the neon lighting, he feels his very soul to be under attack. The building, a featureless block of concrete and glass, seems to give off a gas, odourless, colourless, that finds its way into his blood and numbs him. IBM, he can swear, is killing him, turning him into a zombie.

Yet he cannot give up. Barnet Hill Secondary Modern, Rothamsted, IBM: he dare not fail for a third time. Failing would be too much like his father. Through the grey, heartless agency of IBM the real world is testing him. He must steel himself to endure.

SIX

HIS REFUGE FROM IBM is the cinema. At the Everyman in Hampstead his eyes are opened to films from all over the world, made by directors whose names are quite new to him. He goes to the whole of an Antonioni season. In a film called *L'Eclisse* a woman wanders through the streets of a sunstruck, deserted city. She is disturbed, anguished. What she is anguished about he cannot quite define; her face reveals nothing.

The woman is Monica Vitti. With her perfect legs and sensual lips and abstracted look, Monica Vitti haunts him; he falls in love with her. He has dreams in which he, of all men in the world, is singled out to be her comfort and solace. There is a tap at his door. Monica Vitti stands before him, a finger raised to her lips to signal silence. He steps forward, enfolds her in his arms. Time ceases; he and Monica Vitti are one.

But is he truly the lover Monica Vitti seeks? Will he be any better than the men in her films at stilling her anguish? He is not sure. Even if he found a room for the two of them, a secret retreat in some quiet, fogbound quarter of London, he suspects she would still, at three in the morning, slip out of bed and sit at the table under the glare of a single lamp, brooding, prey to anguish.

The anguish with which Monica Vitti and other of Antonioni's characters are burdened is of a kind he is quite unfamiliar with. In fact it is not anguish at all but something more profound: Angst. He would like to have a taste of Angst, if only to know what it is like. But, try though he may, he cannot find anything in his heart that he can recognize as Angst. Angst seems to be a European, a properly European, thing; it has yet to find its way to England, to say nothing of England's colonies.

In an article in the *Observer*, the Angst of the European cinema is explained as stemming from a fear of nuclear annihilation; also from uncertainty following the death of God. He is not convinced. He cannot believe that what sends Monica Vitti out into the streets of Palermo under the angry red ball of the sun, when she could just as well stay behind in the cool of a hotel room and be made love to by a man, is the hydrogen bomb or a failure on God's part to speak to her. Whatever the true explanation, it must be more complicated than that.

Angst gnaws at Bergman's people too. It is the cause of their irremediable solitariness. Regarding Bergman's Angst, however, the *Observer* recommends that it not be taken too seriously. It smells of pretentiousness, says the *Observer*; it is an affectation not unconnected with long Nordic winters, nights of excessive drinking, hangovers.

Even newspapers that are supposed to be liberal – the *Guardian*, the *Observer* – are hostile, he is beginning to find, to the life of the mind. Faced with something deep and serious, they are quick to sneer, to brush it off with a witticism. Only in tiny enclaves like the Third Programme is new art – American poetry, electronic music, abstract expressionism – taken seriously. Modern England is turning out to be a disturbingly philistine country, little different from the England of W. H. Henley and the *Pomp and Circumstance* marches that Ezra Pound was fulminating against in 1912.

What then is he doing in England? Was it a huge mistake to have come here? Is it too late to move? Would Paris, city of artists, be more congenial, if somehow he could master French? And what of Stockholm? Spiritually he would feel at home in Stockholm, he suspects. But what about Swedish? And what would he do for a living?

At IBM he has to keep his fantasies of Monica Vitti to himself, and the rest of his arty pretensions too. For reasons that are not clear to him, he has been adopted as a chum by a fellow programmer named Bill Briggs. Bill Briggs is short and pimply; he has a girlfriend named Cynthia whom he is going to marry; he is looking forward to making the down payment on a terrace house in Wimbledon. Whereas the other programmers speak with unplaceable grammar-school accents and start the day by flipping to the financial pages of the *Telegraph* to check the share prices, Bill Briggs has a marked London accent and stores his money in a building society account.

Despite his social origins, there is no reason why Bill Briggs should not succeed in IBM. IBM is an American company, impatient of Britain's class hierarchy. That is the strength of IBM: men of all kinds can get to the top because all that matters to IBM is loyalty and hard, concentrated work. Bill Briggs is hardworking, and unquestioningly loyal to IBM. Furthermore, Bill Briggs seems to have a grasp of the larger goals of IBM and of its Newman Street data-processing centre, which is more than can be said of him.

IBM employees are provided with booklets of luncheon vouchers. For a three-and-sixpenny voucher one can get a quite decent meal. His own inclination is toward the Lyons brasserie on Tottenham Court Road, where one can visit the salad bar as often as one likes. But Schmidt's in Charlotte Street is the preferred haunt of the IBM programmers. So with Bill Briggs he goes to Schmidt's and eats Wiener Schnitzel or jugged hare. For variety they sometimes go to the Athena on Goodge Street for moussaka. After lunch, if it is not raining, they take a brief stroll around the streets before returning to their desks.

The range of subjects that he and Bill Briggs have tacitly agreed not to broach in their conversations is so wide that he is surprised there is anything left. They do not discuss their desires or larger aspirations. They are silent on their personal lives, on their families and their upbringing, on politics and religion and the arts. Football would be acceptable were it not for the fact that he knows nothing about the English clubs. So they are left with the weather, train strikes, house prices, and IBM: IBM's plans for the future, IBM's customers and those customers' plans, who said what at IBM.

It makes for dreary conversation, but there is an obverse to it. A bare two months ago he was an ignorant provincial stepping ashore into the drizzle of Southampton docks. Now here he is in the heart of London town, indistinguishable in his black uniform from any other London office-worker, exchanging opinions on everyday subjects with a fullblooded Londoner, successfully negotiating all the conversational proprieties. Soon, if his progress continues and he is careful with his vowels, no one will be sparing him a second glance. In a crowd he will pass as a Londoner, perhaps even, in due course, as an Englishman.

Now that he has an income, he is able to rent a room of his own in a house off Archway Road in north London. The room is on the second floor, with a view over a water reservoir. It has a gas heater and a little alcove with a gas cooker and shelves for food and crockery. In a corner is the meter: you put in a shilling and get a shilling's supply of gas.

His diet is unvarying: apples, oats porridge, bread and cheese, and spiced sausages called chipolatas, which he fries over the cooker. He prefers chipolatas to real sausages because they do not need to be refrigerated. Nor do they ooze grease when they fry. He suspects there is lots of potato flour mixed in with the ground meat. But potato flour is not bad for one.

Since he leaves early in the mornings and comes home late, he rarely lays eyes on the other lodgers. A routine soon sets in. He spends Saturdays in bookshops, galleries, museums, cinemas. On Sundays he reads the *Observer* in his room, then goes to a film or for a walk on the Heath.

Saturday and Sunday evenings are the worst. Then the loneliness that he usually manages to keep at bay sweeps over him, loneliness indistinguishable from the low, grey, wet weather of London or from the iron-hard cold of the pavements. He can feel his face turning stiff and stupid with muteness; even IBM and its formulaic exchanges are better than this silence.

His hope is that from the featureless crowds amidst which he moves there will emerge a woman who will respond to his glance, glide wordlessly to his side, return with him (still wordless – what could their first word be? – it is unimaginable) to his bedsitter, make love to him, vanish into the darkness, reappear the next night (he will be sitting over his books, there will be a tap at the door), again embrace him, again, on the stroke of midnight, vanish, and so forth, thereby transforming his life and releasing a torrent of pent-up verse on the pattern of Rilke's *Sonnets to Orpheus*.

A letter arrives from the University of Cape Town. On the strength of his Honours examinations, it says, he has been awarded a bursary of two hundred pounds for postgraduate study.

The amount is too small, far too small, to allow him to enrol at an English university. Anyhow, now that he has found a job he cannot think of giving it up. Short of refusing the bursary, there is only one option left: to register with the University of Cape Town as a Master's student *in absentia*. He completes the registration form. Under 'Area of Concentration' he writes, after due thought, 'Literature.' It would nice to write 'Mathematics,' but the truth is that he is not clever enough to go on with mathematics. Literature may not be as noble as mathematics, but at least there is nothing about literature that intimidates him. As for the topic of his research, he toys with the idea of proposing the *Cantos* of Ezra Pound, but in the end goes for the novels of Ford Madox Ford. To read Ford one does at least not need to know Chinese.

Ford, born Hueffer, grandson of the painter Ford Madox Brown, published his first book in 1891 at the age of eighteen. From then on, until his death in 1939, he earned his bread solely by literary pursuits. Pound called him the greatest prose stylist of his day and excoriated the English public for ignoring him. He himself has thus far read five of Ford's novels — *The Good Soldier* and the four books constituting *Parade's End* — and is convinced that Pound is right. He is dazzled by the complicated, staggered chronology of Ford's plots, by the cunning with which a note, casually struck and artlessly repeated, will stand revealed, chapters later, as a major motif. He is moved too by the love between Christopher Tietjens and the much younger Valentine Wannop, a love which Tietjens abstains from consummating, despite Valentine's readiness, because (says Tietjens) a fellow doesn't go about deflowering virgins. Tietjens's ethos of laconic common decency seems to him wholly admirable, the quintessence of Englishness.

If Ford could write five such masterpieces, he tells himself, surely there must be further masterworks, as yet unrecognized, among the sprawling and only just catalogued corpus of his writings, masterworks that he can help bring to light. He embarks at once on a reading of the Ford oeuvre, spending entire Saturdays in the Reading Room of the British Museum, as well as the two evenings a week when the Reading Room stays open late. Though the early works turn out to be disappointing, he presses on, excusing Ford because he must still have been learning his craft.

One Saturday he falls into conversation with the reader at the next desk, and they have tea together in the Museum tea-room. Her name is Anna; she is Polish by origin and still has a faint accent. She works as a researcher, she tells him; visits to the Reading Room are part of her job. She is at present exploring materials for a life of John Speke, discoverer of the source of the Nile. For his part, he tells her about Ford and Ford's collaboration with Joseph Conrad. They talk about Conrad's time in Africa, about his early life in Poland and his later aspiration to become an English squire.

As they speak he wonders: Is it an omen that in the Reading Room of the British Museum he, a student of F. M. Ford, should meet a countrywoman of Conrad's? Is Anna his Destined One? She is no beauty, certainly: she is older than he; her face is bony, even gaunt; she wears sensible flat shoes and a shapeless grey skirt. But who is to say that he deserves better?

He is on the point of asking her out, perhaps to a film; but his courage fails him. What if, even when he has declared himself, there is no spark? How would he extricate himself without ignominy?

There are other habitués of the Reading Room as lonely, he suspects, as he. An Indian with a pitted face, for instance, who gives off a smell of boils and old bandages. Every time he goes to the toilet the Indian seems to follow him, to be on the point of speaking, but then unable to.

At last, one day, as they stand side by side at the washbasin, the man speaks. Is he from King's College, the man asks stiffly? No, he replies, from the University of Cape Town. Would he like to have tea, asks the man?

They sit down together in the tearoom; the man launches into a long account of his research, which is into the social makeup of audiences at the Globe Theatre. Though he is not particularly interested, he does his best to pay attention.

The life of the mind, he thinks to himself: is that what we have dedicated ourselves to, I and these other lonely wanderers in the bowels of the British Museum? Will there be a reward for us one day? Will our solitariness lift, or is the life of the mind its own reward?

SEVEN

IT IS THREE o'clock on a Saturday afternoon. He has been in the Reading Room since opening time, reading Ford's *Mr Humpty Dumpty*, a novel so tedious that he has to fight to stay awake.

In a short while the Reading Room will close for the day, the whole great Museum will close. On Sundays the Reading Room does not open; between now and next Saturday, reading will be a matter of an hour snatched here and there of an evening. Should he soldier on until closing time, though he is racked with yawns? What is the point of this enterprise anyway? What is the good to a computer programmer, if computer programming is to be his life, to have an MA in English literature? And where are the unrecognized masterpieces that he was going to uncover? *Mr Humpty Dumpty* is certainly not one of them. He shuts the book, packs up.

Outside the daylight is already waning. Along Great Russell Street he trudges to Tottenham Court Road, then south toward Charing Cross. Of the throng on the sidewalks, most are young people. Strictly speaking he is their contemporary, but he does not feel like that. He feels middle-aged, prematurely middle-aged: one of those bloodless, high-domed, exhausted scholars whose skin flakes at the merest touch. Deeper than that he is still a child, ignorant of his place in the world, frightened, indecisive. What is he doing in this huge, cold city where merely to stay alive means holding tight all the time, trying not to fall?

The bookshops on Charing Cross Road stay open until six. Until six he has somewhere to go. After that he will be adrift amid the Saturday-night fun-seekers. For a while he can follow the flow, pretending he too is seeking fun, pretending he has somewhere to go, someone to meet; but in the end he will have to give up and catch the train back to Archway station and the solitude of his room.

Foyles, the bookshop whose name is known as far away as Cape Town, has proved a disappointment. The boast that Foyles stocks every book in print is clearly a lie, and anyway the assistants, most of them younger than himself, don't know where to find things. He prefers Dillons, haphazard though the shelving at Dillons may be. He tries to call in there once a week to see what is new.

Among the magazines he comes across in Dillons is *The African Communist*. He has heard about *The African Communist* but not actually seen it hitherto, since it is banned in South Africa. Of the contributors, some, to his surprise, turn out to be contemporaries of his from Cape Town – fellow students of the kind who slept all day and went to parties in the evenings, got drunk, sponged on their parents, failed examinations, took five years over their three-year degrees. Yet here they are writing authoritative-sounding articles about the economics of migratory labour or uprisings in rural Transkei. Where, amid all the dancing and drinking and debauchery, did they find the time to learn about such things?

What he really comes to Dillons for, however, are the poetry magazines. There is a careless stack of them on the floor behind the front door: *Ambit* and *Agenda* and *Pawn*; cyclostyled leaflets from out-of-the-way places like Keele; odd numbers, long out of date, of reviews from America. He buys one of each and takes the pile back to his room, where he pores over them, trying to work out who is writing what, where he would fit in if he too were to try to publish.

The British magazines are dominated by dismayingly modest little poems about everyday thoughts and experiences, poems that would not have raised an eyebrow half a century ago. What has happened to the ambitions of poets here in Britain? Have they not digested the news that Edward Thomas and his world are gone for ever? Have they not learned the lesson of Pound and Eliot, to say nothing of Baudelaire and Rimbaud, the Greek epigrammatists, the Chinese?

But perhaps he is judging the British too hastily. Perhaps he is reading the wrong magazines; perhaps there are other, more adventurous publications that do not find their way to Dillons. Or perhaps there is a circle of creative spirits so pessimistic about the prevailing climate that they do not bother to send to bookshops like Dillons the magazines in which they publish. *Botthege Oscure*, for instance: where does one buy *Botthege Oscure*? If such enlightened circles exist, how will he ever find out about them, how will he ever break into them?

As for his own writing, he would hope to leave behind, were he to die tomorrow, a handful of poems that, edited by some selfless scholar and privately printed in a neat little duodecimo pamphlet, would make people shake their heads and murmur beneath their breath, 'Such promise! Such a waste!' That is his hope. The truth, however, is that the poems he writes are becoming not only shorter and shorter but – he cannot help feeling – less substantial too. He no longer seems to have it in him to produce poetry of the kind he wrote at the age of seventeen or eighteen, pieces sometimes pages long, rambling, clumsy in parts, but daring nevertheless, full of novelties. Those poems, or most of them, came out of a state of anguished being-in-love, as well as out of the torrents of reading he was doing. Now, four years later, he is still anguished, but his anguish has become habitual, even chronic, like a headache that will not go away. The poems he writes are wry little pieces, *minor* in every sense. Whatever their nominal subject, it is he himself – trapped, lonely, miserable – who is at their centre; yet – he cannot fail to see it – these new poems lack the energy or even the desire to explore his impasse of spirit seriously.

In fact he is exhausted all the time. At his grey-topped desk in the big IBM office he is overcome with gales of yawning that he struggles to conceal; at the British Museum the words swim before his eyes. All he wants to do is sink his head on his arms and sleep.

Yet he cannot accept that the life he is leading here in London is without plan or meaning. A century ago poets deranged themselves with opium or alcohol so that from the brink of madness they could issue reports on their visionary experiences. By such means they turned themselves into seers, prophets of the future. Opium and alcohol are not his way, he is too frightened of what they might do to his health. But are exhaustion and misery not capable of performing the same work? Is living on the brink of psychic collapse not as good as living on the brink of madness? Why is it a greater sacrifice, a greater extinction of personality, to hide out in a garret room on the Left Bank for which you have not paid the rent, or wander from café to café, bearded, unwashed, smelly, bumming drinks from friends, than to dress in a black suit and do soul-destroying office-work and submit to either loneliness unto death or sex without desire? Surely absinthe and tattered clothes are old-fashioned by now. And what is heroic, anyway, about cheating a landlord out of his rent?

T. S. Eliot worked for a bank. Wallace Stevens and Franz Kafka worked for insurance companies. In their unique ways Eliot and Stevens and Kafka suffered no less than Poe or Rimbaud. There is no dishonour in electing to follow Eliot and Stevens and Kafka. His choice is to wear a black suit as they did, wear it like a burning shirt, exploiting no one, cheating no one, paying his way. In the Romantic era artists went mad on an extravagant scale. Madness poured out of them in reams of delirious verse or great gouts of paint. That era is over: his own madness, if it is to be his lot to suffer madness, will be otherwise – quiet, discreet. He will sit in a corner, tight and hunched, like the robed man in Dürer's etching, waiting patiently for his season in hell to pass. And when it has passed he will be all the stronger for having endured.

That is the story he tells himself on his better days. On other days, bad days, he wonders whether emotions as monotonous as his will ever fuel great poetry. The musical impulse within him, once so strong, has already waned. Is he now in the process of losing the poetic impulse? Will he be driven from poetry to prose? Is that what prose secretly is: the second-best choice, the resort of failing creative spirits?

The only poem he has written in the past year that he likes is a mere five lines long.

The wives of the rock-lobster fishermen
have grown accustomed to waking alone,
their husbands having for centuries fished at dawn;
nor is their sleep as troubled as mine.
If you have gone, go then to the Portuguese rock-lobster
    fishermen.

The Portuguese rock-lobster fishermen: he is quietly pleased to have sneaked so mundane a phrase into a poem, even if the poem itself, looked at closely, makes less and less sense. He has lists of words and phrases he has stored up, mundane or recondite, waiting to find homes for them. *Perfervid*, for instance: one day he will lodge *perfervid* in an epigram whose occult history will be that it will have been created as a setting for a single word, as a brooch can be a setting for a single jewel. The poem will seem to be about love or despair, yet it will all have blossomed out of one lovely-sounding word of whose meaning he is as yet not entirely sure.

Will epigrams be enough to build a career in poetry on? As a form there is nothing wrong with the epigram. A world of feeling can be compressed into a single line, as the Greeks proved again and again. But his epigrams do not always achieve a Greek compression. Too often they lack feeling; too often they are merely bookish.

'Poetry is not a turning loose of emotion but an escape from emotion,' says Eliot in words he has copied into his diary. 'Poetry is not an expression of personality but an escape from personality.' Then as a bitter afterthought Eliot adds: 'But only those who have personality and emotions know what it means to want to escape from these things.'

He has a horror of spilling mere emotion on to the page. Once it has begun to spill out he would not know how to stop it. It would be like severing an artery and watching one's lifeblood gush out. Prose, fortunately, does not demand emotion: there is that to be said for it. Prose is like a flat, tranquil sheet of water on which one can tack about at one's leisure, making patterns on the surface.

He sets aside a weekend for his first experiment with prose. The story that emerges from the experiment, if that is what it is, a story, has no real plot. Everything of importance happens in the mind of the narrator, a nameless young man all too like himself who takes a nameless girl to a lonely beach and watches while she swims. From some small action of hers, some unconscious gesture, he is suddenly convinced she has been unfaithful to him; furthermore, he realizes that she has seen he knows, and does not care. That is all. That is how the piece ends. That is the sum of it.

Having written this story, he does not know what to do with it. He has no urge to show it to anyone except perhaps to the original of the nameless girl. But he has lost touch with her, and she would not recognize herself anyway, not without being prompted.

The story is set in South Africa. It disquiets him to see that he is still writing about South Africa. He would prefer to leave his South African self behind as he has left South Africa itself behind. South Africa was a bad start, a handicap. An undistinguished, rural family, bad schooling, the Afrikaans language: from each of these component handicaps he has, more or less, escaped. He is in the great world earning his own living and not doing too badly, or at least not failing, not obviously. He does not need to be reminded of South Africa. If a tidal wave were to sweep in from the Atlantic tomorrow and wash away the southern tip of the African continent, he will not shed a tear. He will be among the saved.

Though the story he has written is minor (no doubt about that), it is not bad. Nevertheless, he sees no point in trying to publish it. The English will not understand it. For the beach in the story they will summon up an English idea of a beach, a few pebbles lapped by wavelets. They will not see a dazzling space of sand at the foot of rocky cliffs pounded by breakers, with gulls and cormorants screaming overhead as they battle the wind.

There are other ways too, it appears, in which prose is not like poetry. In poetry the action can take place everywhere and nowhere: it does not matter whether the lonely wives of the fishermen live in Kalk Bay or Portugal or Maine. Prose, on the other hand, seems naggingly to demand a specific setting.

He does not as yet know England well enough to do England in prose. He is not even sure he can do the parts of London he is familiar with, the London of crowds trudging to work, of cold and rain, of bedsitters with curtainless windows and forty-watt bulbs. If he were to try, what would come out would be no different, he suspects, from the London of any other bachelor clerk. He may have his own vision of London, but there is nothing unique to that vision. If it has a certain intensity, that is only because it is narrow, and it is narrow because it is ignorant of everything outside itself. He has not mastered London. If there is any mastering going on, it is London mastering him.

EIGHT

DOES HIS FIRST venture into prose herald a change of direction in his life? Is he about to renounce poetry? He is not sure. But if he is going to write prose then he may have to go the whole hog and become a Jamesian. Henry James shows one how to rise above mere nationality. In fact, it is not always clear where a piece by James is set, in London or Paris or New York, so supremely above the mechanics of daily life is James. People in James do not have to pay the rent; they certainly do not have to hold down jobs; all they are required to do is to have super-subtle conversations whose effect is to bring about tiny shifts of power, shifts so minute as to be invisible to all but the practised eye. When enough such shifts have taken place, the balance of power between the personages of the story is (*Voilà!*) revealed to have suddenly and irreversibly changed. And that is that: the story has fulfilled its charge and can be brought to an end.

He sets himself exercises in the style of James. But the Jamesian manner proves less easy to master than he had thought. Getting the characters he dreams up to have supersubtle conversations is like trying to make mammals fly. For a moment or two, flapping their arms, they support themselves in thin air. Then they plunge.

Henry James's sensibility is finer than his, there can be no doubt about that. But that does not explain the whole of his failure. James wants one to believe that conversations, exchanges of words, are all that matters. Though it is a credo he is ready to accept, he cannot follow it, he finds, not in London, the city on whose grim cogs he is being broken, the city from which he must learn to write, otherwise why is he here at all?

Once upon a time, when he was still an innocent child, he believed that cleverness was the only yardstick that mattered, that as long as he was clever enough he would attain everything he desired. Going to university put him in his place. The university showed him he was not the cleverest, not by a long chalk. And now he is faced with real life, where there are not even examinations to fall back on. In real life all that he can do well, it appears, is be miserable. In misery he is still top of the class. There seems to be no limit to the misery he can attract to himself and endure. Even as he plods around the cold streets of this alien city, heading nowhere, just walking to tire himself out, so that when he gets back to his room he will at least be able to sleep, he does not sense within himself the slightest disposition to crack under the weight of misery. Misery is his element. He is at home in misery like a fish in water. If misery were to be abolished, he would not know what to do with himself.

Happiness, he tells himself, teaches one nothing. Misery, on the other hand, steels one for the future. Misery is a school for the soul. From the waters of misery one emerges on the far bank purified, strong, ready to take up again the challenges of a life of art.

Yet misery does not feel like a purifying bath. On the contrary, it feels like a pool of dirty water. From each new bout of misery he emerges not brighter and stronger but duller and flabbier. How does it actually work, the cleansing action that misery is reputed to have? Has he not swum deep enough? Will he have to swim beyond mere misery into melancholia and madness? He has never yet met anyone who could be called properly mad, but he has not forgotten Jacqueline, who was, as she herself put it, 'in therapy,' and with whom he spent six months, on and off, sharing a one-room flat. At no time did Jacqueline blaze with the divine and exhilarating fire of creativity. On the contrary, she was self-obsessed, unpredictable, exhausting to be with. Is that the kind of person he must descend to being before he can be an artist? And anyway, whether mad or miserable, how can one write when tiredness is like a gloved hand gripping one's brain and squeezing? Or is what he likes to call tiredness in fact a test, a disguised test, a test he is moreover failing? After tiredness, are there further tests to come, as many as there are circles in Dante's Hell? Is tiredness simply the first of the tests that the great masters had to pass, Hölderlin and Blake, Pound and Eliot?

He wishes it could be granted to him to come alive and just for a minute, just for a second, know what it is to burn with the sacred fire of art.

Suffering, madness, sex: three ways of calling down the sacred fire upon oneself. He has visited the lower reaches of suffering, he has been in touch with madness; what does he know of sex? Sex and creativity go together, everyone says so, and he does not doubt it. Because they are creators, artists possess the secret of love. The fire that burns in the artist is visible to women, by means of an instinctive faculty. Women themselves do not have the sacred fire (there are exceptions: Sappho, Emily Brontë). It is in quest of the fire they lack, the fire of love, that women pursue artists and give themselves to them. In their lovemaking artists and their mistresses experience briefly, tantalizingly, the life of gods. From such lovemaking the artist returns to his work enriched and strengthened, the woman to her life transfigured.

What of him then? If no woman has yet detected, behind his

woodenness, his clenched grimness, any flicker of the sacred fire; if no woman seems to give herself to him without the severest qualms; if the lovemaking he is familiar with, the woman's as well as his own, is either anxious or bored or both anxious and bored – does it mean that he is not a real artist, or does it mean that he has not suffered enough yet, not spent enough time in a purgatory that includes by prescription bouts of passionless sex?

With his lofty unconcern for mere living, Henry James exerts a strong pull on him. Yet, try though he may, he cannot feel the ghostly hand of James extended to touch his brow in blessing. James belongs to the past: by the time he himself was born, James had been dead for twenty years. James Joyce was still alive, though only by a whisker. He admires Joyce, he can even recite passages from *Ulysses* by heart. But Joyce is too bound up with Ireland and Irish affairs to be in his pantheon. Ezra Pound and T. S. Eliot, tottering though they may be, and myth-shrouded, are still alive, the one in Rapallo, the other here in London. But if he is going to abandon poetry (or poetry is going to abandon him), what example can Pound or Eliot any longer offer?

Of the great figures of the present age, that leaves only one: D. H. Lawrence. Lawrence too died before he was born, but that can be discounted as an accident, since Lawrence died young. He first read Lawrence as a schoolboy, when *Lady Chatterley's Lover* was the most notorious of all forbidden books. By his third year at university he had consumed the whole of Lawrence, save for the apprentice work. Lawrence was being absorbed by his fellow students too. From Lawrence they were learning to smash the brittle shell of civilized convention and let the secret core of their being emerge. Girls wore flowing dresses and danced in the rain and gave themselves to men who promised to take them to their dark core. Men who failed to take them there they impatiently discarded.

He himself had been wary of becoming a cultist, a Lawrentian. The women in Lawrence's books made him uneasy; he imagined them as remorseless female insects, spiders or mantises. Under the gaze of the pale, black-clad, intent-eyed priestesses of the cult at the university he felt like a nervous, scurrying little bachelor insect. With some of them he would have liked to go to bed, that he could not deny – only by bringing a woman to her own dark core, after all, could a man reach his own dark core – but he was too scared. Their ecstasies would be volcanic; he would be too puny to survive them.

Besides, women who followed Lawrence had a code of chastity of their own. They fell into long periods of iciness during which they wished only to be by themselves or with their sisters, periods during which the thought of offering up their bodies was like a violation. From their icy sleep they could be awoken only by the imperious call of the dark male self. He himself was neither dark nor imperious, or at least his essential darkness and imperiousness had yet to emerge. So he made do with other girls, girls who had not yet become women and might never become women, since they had no dark core or none to speak of, girls who in their hearts didn't want to do it, just as in his heart of hearts he could not have been said to want to do it either.

In his last weeks in Cape Town he had begun an affair with a girl named Caroline, a drama student with stage ambitions. They had gone to the theatre together, they had stayed up all night arguing the merits of Anouilh as against Sartre, Ionesco as against Beckett; they had slept together. Beckett was his favourite but not Caroline's: Beckett was too gloomy, she said. Her real reason, he suspected, was that Beckett did not write parts for

68

women. At her prodding he had even embarked on a play himself, a verse drama about Don Quixote. But he soon found himself at a dead end – the mind of the old Spaniard was too remote, he could not think his way into it – and gave up.

Now, months later, Caroline turns up in London and gets in touch with him. They meet in Hyde Park. She still has a southern-hemisphere tan, she is full of vitality, elated to be in London, elated too to see him. They stroll through the park. Spring has arrived, the evenings are growing longer, there are leaves on the trees. They catch a bus back to Kensington, where she lives.

He is impressed by her, by her energy and enterprise. A few weeks in London and she has already found her feet. She has a job; her CV has gone out to all the theatrical agents; and she has a flat in a fashionable quarter, which she shares with three English girls. How did she meet her flat-mates, he asks? Friends of friends, she replies.

They resume their affair, but it is difficult from the start. The job she has found is as a waitress in a nightclub in the West End; the hours are unpredictable. She prefers that he meet her at her flat, not fetch her at the club. Since the other girls object to strangers having keys, he has to wait outside in the street. So at the end of his own working day he catches a train back to Archway Road, has a supper of bread and sausages in his room, reads for an hour or two or listens to the radio, then catches the last bus to Kensington and begins his wait. Sometimes Caroline comes back from the club as early as midnight, sometimes as late as 4 a.m. They have their time together, fall asleep. At seven o'clock the alarm clock rings: he must be out of the flat before her friends wake up. He catches the bus back to Highgate, has breakfast, dons his black uniform, and sets off for the office.

It soon becomes a routine, a routine which, when he is able

to stand back for a moment and reflect, astonishes him. He is having an affair in which the rules are being set by the woman and by the woman alone. Is this what passion does to a man: robs him of his pride? Is he passionate about Caroline? He would not have imagined so. In the time they were apart he barely gave her a thought. Why then this docility on his part, this abjectness? Does he want to be made unhappy? Is that what unhappiness has become for him: a drug he cannot do without?

Worst are the nights when she does not come home at all. He paces the sidewalk hour after hour, or, when it rains, huddles in the doorway. Is she really working late, he wonders despairingly, or is the club in Bayswater a huge lie and is she at this very moment in bed with someone else?

When he taxes her directly, he gets only vague excuses. It was a hectic night at the club, we stayed open till dawn, she says. Or she didn't have cash for a taxi. Or she had to go for a drink with a client. In the acting world, she reminds him tartly, contacts are all-important. Without contacts her career will never take off.

They still make love, but it is not as it was before. Caroline's mind is elsewhere. Worse than that: with his glooms and his sulks he is fast becoming a burden to her, he can feel that. If he had any sense he would break off the affair right now, clear out. But he does not. Caroline may not be the mysterious, dark-eyed beloved he came to Europe for, she may be nothing but a girl from Cape Town from a background as humdrum as his own, but she is, for the present, all he has.

NINE

IN ENGLAND GIRLS pay no attention to him, perhaps because there still lingers about his person an air of colonial gaucherie, perhaps simply because his clothes are not right. When he is not dressed up in one of his IBM suits, he has only the grey flannels and green sports jacket he brought with him from Cape Town. The young men he sees in the trains and the streets, in contrast, wear narrow black trousers, pointed shoes, tight, boxlike jackets with many buttons. They also wear their hair long, hanging over their foreheads and ears, while he still has the short back and sides and the neat parting impressed on him in his childhood by country-town barbers and approved of by IBM. In the trains the eyes of girls slide over him or glaze with disdain.

There is something not quite fair in his plight: he would protest if he only knew where and to whom. What kind of jobs do his rivals have that allow them to dress as they please? And why should he be compelled to follow fashion anyway? Do inner qualities count for nothing?

The sensible thing would be to buy himself an outfit like theirs and wear it at weekends. But when he imagines dressing up in such clothes, clothes that seem to him not only alien to his character but Latin rather than English, he feels his resistance stiffening. He cannot do it: it would be like giving himself up to a charade, an act.

London is full of beautiful girls. They come from all over the world: as au pairs, as language students, simply as tourists. They wear their hair in wings over their cheekbones; their eyes are dark-shadowed; they have an air of suave mystery. The most beautiful are the tall, honey-skinned Swedes; but the Italians, almond-eyed and petite, have their own allure. Italian lovemaking, he imagines, will be sharp and hot, quite different from Swedish, which will be smiling and languorous. But will he ever get a chance to find out for himself? If he could ever pluck up the courage to speak to one of these beautiful foreigners, what would he say? Would it be a lie if he introduced himself as a mathematician rather than just a computer programmer? Would the attentions of a mathematician impress a girl from Europe, or would it be better to tell her that, despite his dull exterior, he is a poet?

He carries a book of poetry around with him in his pocket, sometimes Hölderlin, sometimes Rilke, sometimes Vallejo. In the trains he ostentatiously brings forth his book and absorbs himself in it. It is a test. Only an exceptional girl will appreciate what he is reading and recognize in him an exceptional spirit too. But none of the girls on the trains pay him any attention. That seems to be one of the first things girls learn when they arrive in England: to pay no attention to signals from men.

What we call beauty is simply a first intimation of terror, Rilke tells him. We prostrate ourselves before beauty to thank it for disdaining to destroy us. Would they destroy him if he ventured too close, these beautiful creatures from other worlds, these angels, or would they find him too negligible for that?

In a poetry magazine – *Ambit* perhaps, or *Agenda* – he finds an announcement for a weekly workshop run by the Poetry

Society for the benefit of young, unpublished writers. He turns up at the advertised time and place wearing his black suit. The woman at the door inspects him suspiciously, demands his age. 'Twenty-one,' he says. It is a lie: he is twenty-two.

Sitting around in leather armchairs, his fellow poets eye him, nod distantly. They seem to know one another; he is the only newcomer. They are younger than he, teenagers in fact, except for a middle-aged man with a limp who is something in the Poetry Society. They take turns to read out their latest poems. The poem he himself reads ends with the words 'the furious waves of my incontinence.' The man with the limp deems his word-choice unfortunate. To anyone who has worked in a hospital, he says, incontinence means urinary incontinence or worse.

He turns up again the next week, and after the session has coffee with a girl who has read out a poem about the death of a friend in a car accident, a good poem in its way, quiet, unpretentious. When she is not writing poetry, the girl informs him, she is a student at King's College, London; she dresses with appropriate severity in dark skirt and black stockings. They arrange to meet again.

They meet at Leicester Square on a Saturday afternoon. They had half agreed to go to a film; but as poets they have a duty to life at its fullest, so they repair to her room off Gower Street instead, where she allows him to undress her. He marvels at the shapeliness of her naked body, the ivory whiteness of her skin. Are all Englishwomen as beautiful when their clothes are off, he wonders?

Naked they lie in each other's arms, but there is no warmth between them; and warmth, it becomes clear, will not grow. At last the girl withdraws, folds her arms across her breasts, pushes his hands away, shakes her head mutely.

He could try to persuade her, induce her, seduce her; he

might even succeed; but he lacks the spirit for it. She is not only a woman, after all, with a woman's intuitions, but an artist too. What he is trying to draw her into is not the real thing – she must know that.

In silence they get dressed. 'I'm sorry,' she says. He shrugs. He is not cross. He does not blame her. He is not without intuitions of his own. The verdict she has delivered on him would be his verdict too.

After this episode he stops going to the Poetry Society. He has never felt welcome there anyway.

He has no further luck with English girls. There are English girls enough at IBM, secretaries and punch operators, and opportunities to chat to them. But from them he feels a certain resistance, as if they are not sure who he is, what his motives might be, what he is doing in their country. He watches them with other men. Other men flirt with them in a jolly, coaxing English way. They respond to being flirted with, he can see that: they open like flowers. But flirting is not something he has learned to do. He is not even sure he approves of it. And anyhow, he cannot let it become known among the IBM girls that he is a poet. They would giggle among themselves, they would spread the story all over the building.

His highest aspiration, higher than for an English girlfriend, higher even than for a Swede or an Italian, is to have a French girl. If he had a passionate affair with a French girl he would be touched and improved, he is sure, by the grace of the French language, the subtlety of French thought. But why should a French girl, any more than an English girl, deign to speak to him? And anyway, he has not so much as laid eyes on a French girl in London. The French have France, after all, the most beautiful country in the world. Why should they come to chilly England to look after the natives' babies?

The French are the most civilized people in the world. All the writers he respects are steeped in French culture; most regard France as their spiritual home – France and, to an extent, Italy, though Italy seems to have fallen on hard times. Since the age of fifteen, when he sent off a postal order for five pounds ten shillings to the Pelman Institute and received in return a grammar book and a set of exercise sheets to be completed and returned to the Institute for marking, he has been trying to learn French. In his trunk, brought all the way from Cape Town, he has the five hundred cards on which he wrote out a basic French vocabulary, one word per card, to carry around and memorize; through his mind runs a patter of French locutions – *je viens de*, I have just; *il me faut*, I must.

But his efforts have got him nowhere. He has no feel for French. Listening to French language records he cannot, most of the time, tell where one word ends and the next begins. Though he can read simple prose texts, he cannot in his inner ear hear what they sound like. The language resists him, excludes him; he cannot find a way in.

In theory he ought to find French easy. He knows Latin; for the pleasure of it he sometimes reads passages of Latin aloud – not the Latin of the Golden or the Silver Age but the Latin of the Vulgate, with its brash disregard for classical word-order. He picks up Spanish without difficulty. He reads Cesar Vallejo in a dual-language text, reads Nicolas Guillén, reads Pablo Neruda. Spanish is full of barbaric-sounding words whose meaning he cannot even guess at, but that does not matter. At least every letter is pronounced, down to the double *r*.

The language for which he has a real feeling, however, is German. He tunes in to broadcasts from Cologne and, when they are not too tedious, from East Berlin as well, and for the most part understands them; he reads German poetry and follows

it well enough. He approves of the way in which every sylla-
ble in German is given its due weight. With the ghost of Afrikaans
still in his ears, he is at home in the syntax. In fact, he takes
pleasure in the length of German sentences, in the complex
pileup of verbs at the end. There are times, reading German,
when he forgets he is in a foreign language.

He reads Ingeborg Bachmann over and over; he reads Bertolt
Brecht, Hans Magnus Enzensberger. There is a sardonic under-
current in German that attracts him though he is not sure he
quite grasps why it is there – indeed wonders whether he is not
just imagining it. He could ask, but he knows no one else who
reads German poetry, just as he knows no one who speaks
French.

Yet in this huge city there must be thousands of people steeped
in German literature, thousands more who read poetry in
Russian, Hungarian, Greek, Italian – read it, translate it, even
write it: poets in exile, men with long hair and hornrimmed
glasses, women with sharp foreign faces and full, passionate lips.
In the magazines he buys at Dillons he finds evidence enough
of their existence: translations that must be their handiwork. But
how will he ever meet them? What do they do, these special
beings, when they are not reading and writing and translating?
Does he, unbeknown to himself, sit amongst them in the audi-
ence at the Everyman, walk amongst them on Hampstead Heath?

On an impulse he strolls behind a likely-looking couple on
the Heath. The man is tall and bearded, the woman has long
blonde hair swept casually back. He is sure they are Russian.
But when he gets close enough to eavesdrop they turn out to
be English; they are talking about the price of furniture at Heal's.

There remains Holland. At least he has an insider's knowledge of Dutch, at least he has that advantage. Among all the
circles in London, is there a circle of Dutch poets too? If there

is, will his acquaintance with the language give him an entrée to it?

Dutch poetry has always struck him as rather boring, but the name Simon Vinkenoog keeps cropping up in poetry magazines. Vinkenoog is the one Dutch poet who seems to have broken on to the international stage. He reads everything there is by Vinkenoog in the British Museum, and is not encouraged. Vinkenoog's writings are raucous, crass, lacking any dimension of mystery. If Vinkenoog is all that Holland can offer, then his worst suspicion is confirmed: that of all nations the Dutch are the dullest, the most antipoetic. So much for his Netherlandic heritage. He might as well be monolingual.

Every now and again Caroline phones him at work and arranges to meet him. Once they are together, however, she does not conceal her impatience with him. How can he come all the way to London, she says, and then spend his days adding up numbers on a machine? Look around, she says: London is a gallery of novelties and pleasures and amusements. Why does he not come out of himself, have some fun?

'Some of us are not built for fun,' he replies. She takes it as one of his little jokes, does not try to understand.

Caroline has never yet explained where she gets the money for the flat in Kensington and the new outfits she keeps appearing in. Her stepfather in South Africa is in the motor business. Is the motor business lucrative enough to fund a life of pleasure for a stepdaughter in London? What does Caroline actually do at the club where she spends the night hours? Hang coats in the cloakroom and collect tips? Carry trays of drinks? Or is working in a club a euphemism for something else?

Among the contacts she has made at the club, she informs him, is Laurence Olivier. Laurence Olivier is taking an interest in her acting career. He has promised her a part in an as yet unspecified play; he has also invited her to his house in the country.

What must he make of this information? The part in a play sounds like a lie; but is Laurence Olivier lying to Caroline or is Caroline lying to him? Laurence Olivier must by now be an old man with false teeth. Can Caroline take care of herself against Laurence Olivier, if the man who has invited her to his house in the country is indeed Olivier? What do men of that age do with girls for pleasure? Is it appropriate to be jealous of a man who can probably no longer manage an erection? Is jealousy anyhow an out-of-date emotion, here in London in 1962?

Most likely Laurence Olivier, if that is who it is, will give her the full country-house treatment, including a chauffeur to meet her at the station and a butler to wait on them at the dinner table. Then when she is befuddled with claret he will conduct her to his bed and fiddle with her, and she will let it happen, out of politeness, to thank him for the evening, and for the sake of her career too. In their têtes-à-têtes will she bother to mention that there is a rival in the background, a clerk who works for an adding machine company and lives in a room off the Archway Road where he sometimes writes verses?

He does not understand why Caroline does not break off with him, the clerk boyfriend. Creeping home in the early-morning dark after a night with her, he can only pray she will not get in touch with him again. And indeed, a week will sometimes pass with no word from her. Then, just as he is beginning to feel the affair is past history, she will telephone and the cycle will recommence.

He believes in passionate love and its transfiguring power. His experience, however, is that amatory relations devour his time, exhaust him, and cripple his work. Is it possible that he was not made to love women, that in truth he is a homosexual? If he were homosexual, that would explain his woes from beginning to end. Yet ever since he turned sixteen he has been fascinated by the beauty of women, by their air of mysterious unattainability. As a student he was in a continual fever of lovesickness, now for one girl, now for another, sometimes for two at the same time. Reading the poets only heightened his fever. Through the blinding ecstasy of sex, said the poets, one is transported into brightness beyond compare, into the heart of silence; one becomes at one with the elemental forces of the universe. Though brightness beyond compare has eluded him thus far, he does not doubt for a moment that the poets are correct.

One evening he allows himself to be picked up in the street, by a man. The man is older than he – in fact, of another generation. They go by taxi to Sloane Square, where the man lives – it would seem alone – in a flat full of tasselled cushions and dim table-lamps.

They barely talk. He allows the man to touch him through his clothes; he offers nothing in return. If the man has an orgasm, he manages it discreetly. Afterwards he lets himself out and goes home.

Is that homosexuality? Is that the sum of it? Even if there is more to it than that, it seems a puny activity compared with sex with a woman: quick, absent-minded, devoid of dread but also devoid of allure. There seems to be nothing at stake: nothing to lose but nothing to win either. A game for people afraid of the big league; a game for losers.

TEN

THE PLAN AT the back of his mind when he came to England, insofar as he had a plan, had been to find a job and save money. When he had enough money he would give up the job and devote himself to writing. When his savings ran out he would find a new job, and so forth.

He soon discovers how naïve that plan is. His salary at IBM, before deductions, is sixty pounds a month, of which he can save at most ten. A year of labour will earn him two months of freedom; much of that free time will be eaten up in searching for the next job. The scholarship money from South Africa will barely pay his academic fees.

Furthermore, he learns, he is not at liberty to change employers at will. New regulations governing aliens in England specify that each change of employment be approved by the Home Office. It is forbidden to be footloose: if he resigns from IBM he must promptly find other work or else leave the country.

He has been with IBM long enough by now to be habituated to the routine. Yet still he finds the work-day hard to get through. Though he and his fellow programmers are continually urged, at meetings, in memos, to remember they are the cutting edge of the data-processing profession, he feels like a bored clerk in Dickens sitting on a stool, copying musty documents.

The sole interruptions to the tedium of the day come at eleven and three-thirty, when the tea lady arrives with her trolley to slap down a cup of strong English tea before each of them ('There you go, love'). Only when the five o'clock flurry is past – the secretaries and punch operators leave on the dot, no question of overtime with them – and the evening deepens is he free to leave his desk, wander around, relax. The machine room downstairs, dominated by the huge memory cabinets of the 7090, is more often than not empty; he can run programs on the little 1401 computer, even, surreptitiously, play games on it.

At such times he finds his job not just bearable but pleasing. He would not mind spending all night in the bureau, running programs of his own devising until he grows dozy, then brushing his teeth in the toilet and spreading a sleeping-bag under his desk. It would be better than catching the last train and trudging up Archway Road to his lonely room. But such irregular behaviour would be frowned on by IBM.

He makes friends with one of the punch operators. Her name is Rhoda; she is somewhat thick-legged but has an attractively silky olive complexion. She takes her work seriously; sometimes he stands in the doorway watching her, bent over her keyboard. She is aware of him watching but does not seem to mind.

He never gets to talk to Rhoda about anything beyond work. Her English, with its triphthongs and glottal stops, is not easy to follow. She is a native in a way that his fellow programmers, with their grammar-school backgrounds, are not; the life she leads outside work hours is a closed book to him.

He had prepared himself, when he arrived in the country, for the famous British coldness of temperament. But the girls at IBM, he finds, are not like that at all. They have a cosy sensuality of their own, the sensuality of animals brought up together in the same steamy den, familiar with each other's body habits.

81

Though they cannot compete in glamour with the Swedes and Italians, he is attracted to these English girls, to their equability and humorousness. He would like to get to know Rhoda better. But how? She belongs to a foreign tribe. The barriers he would have to work his way past, to say nothing of the conventions of tribal courtship, baffle and dishearten him.

The efficiency of the Newman Street operation is measured by the use it makes of the 7090. The 7090 is the heart of the bureau, the reason for its existence. When the 7090 is not running its time is called idle time. Idle time is inefficient, and inefficiency is a sin. The ultimate goal of the bureau is to keep the 7090 running all day and all night; the most valued clients are those who occupy the 7090 for hours on end. Such clients are the fief of the senior programmers; he has nothing to do with them.

One day, however, one of the serious clients runs into difficulties with his data cards, and he is assigned to help him. The client is a Mr Pomfret, a little man in a rumpled suit and glasses. He comes to London each Thursday from somewhere in the north of England, bringing boxes and boxes of punched cards; he has a regular six-hour booking on the 7090, starting at midnight. From gossip in the office he learns that the cards contain wind-tunnel data for a new British bomber, the TSR-2, being developed for the RAF.

Mr Pomfret's problem, and the problem of Mr Pomfret's colleagues back north, is that the results of the last two weeks' runs are anomalous. They make no sense. Either the test data are faulty or there is something wrong with the design of the plane. His assignment is to reread Mr Pomfret's cards on the auxiliary machine, the 1401, carrying out checks to determine whether any have been mispunched.

He works past midnight. Batch by batch he passes Mr Pomfret's cards through the card-reader. In the end he is able to report there is nothing wrong with the punching. The results were indeed anomalous; the problem is real.

The problem is real. In the most incidental, the most minor way, he has joined the TSR-2 project, become part of the British defence effort; he has furthered British plans to bomb Moscow. Is this what he came to England for: to participate in evil, an evil in which there is no reward, not even the most imaginary? Where is the romance in staying up all night so that Mr Pomfret the aeronautical engineer, with his soft and rather helpless air and his suitcase full of cards, can catch the first train north so as to get to the lab in time for his Friday-morning meeting?

He mentions in a letter to his mother that he has been working on wind-tunnel data for the TSR-2, but his mother has not the faintest idea what the TSR-2 is.

The wind-tunnel tests come to an end. Mr Pomfret's visits to London cease. He watches the papers for further news of the TSR-2, but there is nothing. The TSR-2 seems to have gone into limbo.

Now that it is too late, he wonders what would have happened if, while the TSR-2 cards were in his hands, he had surreptitiously doctored the data on them. Would the whole bomber project have been thrown into confusion, or would the engineers in the north have detected his meddling? On the one hand, he would like to do his bit to save Russia from being bombed. On the other, has he a moral right to enjoy British hospitality while sabotaging their air force? And anyhow, how would the Russians ever get to know that an obscure sympathizer in an IBM office in London had won them a few days' breathing-space in the Cold War?

He does not see what the British have against the Russians. Britain and Russia have been on the same side in all the wars he knows of since 1854. The Russians have never threatened to invade Britain. Why then are the British siding with the Americans, who behave like bullies in Europe as all over the world? It is not as though the British actually like the Americans. Newspaper cartoonists are always taking digs at American tourists, with their cigars and pot-bellies and flowered Hawaiian shirts and the fistfuls of dollars they brandish. In his opinion, the British ought to take their lead from the French and get out of NATO, leaving the Americans and their new chums the West Germans to pursue their grudge against Russia.

The newspapers are full of CND, the Campaign for Nuclear Disarmament. The pictures they print of weedy men and plain girls with ratty hair waving placards and shouting slogans do not predispose him to like CND. On the other hand, Khrushchev has just carried out a tactical masterstroke: he has built Russian missile-pods in Cuba to counteract the American missiles that ring Russia. Now Kennedy is threatening to bombard Russia unless the Russian missiles are removed from Cuba. This is what CND is agitating against: a nuclear strike in which American bases in Britain would participate. He cannot but approve of its stand.

American spy-planes take pictures of Russian freighters crossing the Atlantic on their way to Cuba. The freighters are carrying more missiles, say the Americans. In the pictures the missiles – vague shapes under tarpaulins – are circled in white. In his view, the shapes could just as well be lifeboats. He is surprised that the papers don't question the American story.

Wake up! clamours CND: *we are on the brink of nuclear annihilation.* Might it be true, he wonders? Is everyone going to perish, himself included?

He goes to a big CND rally in Trafalgar Square, taking care to stay on the fringes as a way of signalling that he is only an onlooker. It is the first mass meeting he has ever been to: fist-shaking and slogan-chanting, the whipping up of passion in general, repel him. Only love and art are, in his opinion, worthy of giving oneself to without reserve.

The rally is the culmination of a fifty-mile march by CND stalwarts that started a week ago outside Aldermaston, the British atomic weapons station. For days the *Guardian* has been carrying pictures of sodden marchers on the road. Now, on Trafalgar Square, the mood is dark. As he listens to the speeches it becomes clear that these people, or some of them, do indeed believe what they say. They believe that London is going to be bombed; they believe they are all going to die.

Are they right? If they are, it seems vastly unfair: unfair to the Russians, unfair to the people of London, but unfair most of all to him, having to be incinerated as a consequence of American bellicosity.

He thinks of young Nikolai Rostov on the battlefield of Austerlitz, watching like a hypnotized rabbit as the French grenadiers come charging at him with their grim bayonets. *How can they want to kill me,* he protests to himself – *me, whom everyone is so fond of?*

From the frying-pan into the fire! What an irony! Having escaped the Afrikaners who want to press-gang him into their army and the blacks who want to drive him into the sea, to find himself on an island that is shortly to be turned to cinders! What kind of world is this in which he lives? Where can one turn to be free of the fury of politics? Only Sweden seems to be above the fray. Should he throw up everything and catch the next boat to Stockholm? Does one have to speak Swedish to get into Sweden? Does Sweden need computer programmers? Does Sweden even have computers?

The rally ends. He goes back to his room. He ought to be

reading *The Golden Bowl* or working on his poems, but what would be the point, what is the point of anything?

Then a few days later the crisis is suddenly over. In the face of Kennedy's threats, Khrushchev capitulates. The freighters are ordered to turn back. The missiles already in Cuba are disarmed. The Russians produce a form of words to explain their action, but they have clearly been humiliated. From this episode in history only the Cubans emerge with credit. Undaunted, the Cubans vow that, missiles or not, they will defend their revolution to the last drop of blood. He approves of the Cubans, and of Fidel Castro. At least Fidel is not a coward.

At the Tate Gallery he falls into conversation with a girl he takes to be a tourist. She is plain, bespectacled, solidly planted on her feet, the kind of girl he is not interested in but probably belongs with. Her name is Astrid, she tells him. She is from Austria – from Klagenfurt, not Vienna.

Astrid is not a tourist, it turns out, but an au pair. The next day he takes her to a film. Their tastes are quite dissimilar, he sees that at once. Nevertheless, when she invites him back to the house where she works, he does not say no. He gets a brief glimpse of her room: a garret with blue gingham curtains and matching coverlet and a teddy-bear propped against the pillow.

Downstairs he has tea with her and her employer, an Englishwoman whose cool eyes take his measure and find him wanting. This is a European house, her eyes say: we don't need a graceless colonial here, and a Boer to boot.

It is not a good time to be a South African in England. With great show of self-righteousness, South Africa has declared itself a republic and promptly been expelled from the British Commonwealth. The message contained in that expulsion has been unmistakable. The British have had enough of the Boers and of Boer-led South Africa, a colony that has always been more trouble than it has been worth. They would be content if South Africa would quietly vanish over the horizon. They certainly do not want forlorn South African whites cluttering their doorstep like orphans in search of parents. He has no doubt that Astrid will be obliquely informed by this suave Englishwoman that he is not a desirable.

Out of loneliness, out of pity too, perhaps, for this unhappy, graceless foreigner with her poor English, he invites Astrid out again. Afterwards, for no good reason, he persuades her to come back with him to his room. She is not yet eighteen, still has baby fat on her; he has never been with someone so young – a child, really. Her skin, when he undresses her, feels cold and clammy. He has made a mistake, already he knows it. He feels no desire; as for Astrid, though women and their needs are usually a mystery to him, he is sure she feels none either. But they have come too far, the two of them, to pull back, so they go through with it.

In the weeks that follow they spend several more evenings together. But time is always a problem. Astrid can come out only after her employers' children have been put to bed; they have at most a hurried hour together before the last train back to Kensington. Once she is brave enough to stay the whole night. He pretends to like having her there, but the truth is he does not. He sleeps better by himself. With someone sharing his bed he lies tense and stiff all night, wakes up exhausted.

ELEVEN

YEARS AGO, WHEN he was still a child in a family trying its best
to be normal, his parents used to go to Saturday night dances. He
would watch while they made their preparations; if he stayed up
late enough, he could interrogate his mother afterwards. But what
actually went on in the ballroom of the Masonic Hotel in the
town of Worcester he never got to see: what kind of dances his
parents danced, whether they pretended to gaze into each other's
eyes while they did it, whether they danced only with each other
or whether, as in American films, a stranger was allowed to put a
hand on the woman's shoulder and take her away from her partner, so that the partner would have to find another partner for
himself or else stand in a corner smoking a cigarette and sulking.

Why people who were already married should go to the trouble of dressing up and going to a hotel to dance when they
could have done it just as well in the living room, to music on
the radio, he found hard to understand. But to his mother
Saturday nights at the Masonic Hotel were apparently important, as important as being free to ride a horse or, when no
horse was to be had, a bicycle. Dancing and horseriding stood
for the life that had been hers before she married, before, in her
version of her life-story, she became a prisoner ('I will not be
a prisoner in this house!').

Her adamancy got her nowhere. Whoever it was from his father's office who had given them lifts to the Saturday night dances moved house or stopped going. The shiny blue dress with its silver pin, the white gloves, the funny little hat that sat on the side of the head, vanished into closets and drawers, and that was that.

As for himself, he was glad the dancing had come to an end, though he did not say so. He did not like his mother to go out, did not like the abstracted air that came over her the next day. In dancing itself he saw no sense anyway. Films that promised to have dancing in them he avoided, put off by the goofy, sentimental look that people got on their faces.

'Dancing is good exercise,' insisted his mother. 'It teaches you rhythm and balance.' He was not persuaded. If people needed exercise, they could do calisthenics or swing barbells or run around the block.

In the years that have passed since he left Worcester behind he has not changed his mind about dancing. When as a university student he found it too much of an embarrassment to go to parties and not know how to dance, he enrolled for a package of lessons at a dance school, paying for them out of his own pocket: quickstep, waltz, twist, cha-cha. It did not work: within months he had forgotten everything, in an act of willed forgetting. Why that happened he knows perfectly well. Never for a moment, even during the lessons, was he really giving himself to the dance. Though his feet followed the patterns, inwardly he remained rigid with resistance. And so it still is: at the deepest level he can see no reason why people need to dance.

Dancing makes sense only when it is interpreted as something else, something that people prefer not to admit. That *something else* is the real thing: the dance is merely a cover. Inviting a girl to dance stands for inviting her to have intercourse; accepting the invitation stands for agreeing to have intercourse; and dancing is a miming and foreshadowing of intercourse. So obvious are the correspondences that he wonders why people bother with dancing at all. Why the dressing up, why the ritual motions; why the huge sham?

Old-fashioned dance music with its clodhopping rhythms, the music of the Masonic Hotel, has always bored him. As for the crude music from America to which people of his own age dance, he feels only a fastidious distaste for it.

Back in South Africa the songs on the radio all came from America. In the newspapers the antics of American film stars were obsessively followed, American crazes like the hula hoop slavishly imitated. Why? Why look to America in everything? Disowned by the Dutch and now by the British, had South Africans made up their minds to become fake Americans, even though most had never clapped eyes on a real American in their lives?

In Britain he had expected to get away from America – from American music, American fads. But to his dismay the British are no less eager to ape America. The popular newspapers carry pictures of girls screaming their heads off at concerts. Men with hair down to their shoulders shout and whine in fake American accents and then smash their guitars to pieces. It is all beyond him.

Britain's saving grace is the Third Programme. If there is one thing he looks forward to after a day at IBM, it is coming home to the quiet of his room and switching on the radio and being visited with music he has never heard before, or cool, intelligent talk. Evening after evening, without fail and at no cost, the portals open at his touch.

The Third Programme broadcasts only on long wave. If the Third Programme were on short wave he might have picked it up in Cape Town. In that case, what need would there have been to come to London?

There is a talk in the 'Poets and Poetry' series about a Russian named Joseph Brodsky. Accused of being a social parasite, Joseph Brodsky has been sentenced to five years of hard labour in a camp on the Archangel peninsula in the frozen north. The sentence is still running. Even as he sits in his warm room in London, sipping his coffee, nibbling his dessert of raisins and nuts, there is a man of his own age, a poet like himself, sawing logs all day, nursing frostbitten fingers, patching his boots with rags, living on fish heads and cabbage soup.

'As dark as the inside of a needle,' writes Brodsky in one of his poems. He cannot get the line out of his mind. If he concentrated, truly concentrated, night after night, if he compelled, by sheer attention, the blessing of inspiration to descend upon him, he might be able to come up with something to match it. For he has it in him, he knows, his imagination is of the same colour as Brodsky's. But how to get word through to Archangel afterwards?

On the basis of the poems he has heard on the radio and nothing else, he knows Brodsky, knows him through and through. That is what poetry is capable of. Poetry is truth. But of him in London Brodsky can know nothing. How to tell the frozen man he is with him, by his side, day by day?

Joseph Brodsky, Ingeborg Bachmann, Zbigniew Herbert: from lone rafts tossed on the dark seas of Europe they release their words into the air, and along the airwaves the words speed to his room, the words of the poets of his time, telling him again of what poetry can be and therefore of what he can be, filling him with joy that he inhabits the same earth as they. 'Signal heard in London – please continue to transmit': that is the message he would send them if he could.

In South Africa he had heard one or two pieces by Schoenberg and Berg – *Verklärte Nacht*, the violin concerto. Now for the first time he hears the music of Anton von Webern. He has been warned against Webern. Webern goes too far, he has read: what Webern writes is no longer music, just random sounds. Crouched over the radio, he listens. First one note, then another, then another, cold as ice crystals, strung out like stars in the sky. A minute or two of this raptness, then it is over.

Webern was shot in 1945 by an American soldier. A misunderstanding, it was called, an accident of war. The brain that mapped those sounds, those silences, that sound-and-silence, extinguished for ever.

He goes to an exhibition of the abstract expressionists at the Tate Gallery. For a quarter of an hour he stands before a Jackson Pollock, giving it a chance to penetrate him, trying to look judicious in case some suave Londoner has an eye on this provincial ignoramus. It does not help. The painting means nothing to him. There is something about it he does not get.

In the next room, high up on a wall, sits a huge painting consisting of no more than an elongated black blob on a white field. *Homage to the Spanish Republic 24* by Robert Motherwell, says the label. He is transfixed. Menacing and mysterious, the black shape takes him over. A sound like the stroke of a gong goes out from it, leaving him shaken and weak-kneed.

Where does its power come from, this amorphous shape that bears no resemblance to Spain or anything else, yet stirs up a well of dark feeling within him? It is not beautiful, yet it speaks like beauty, imperiously. Why does Motherwell have this power and not Pollock, or Van Gogh, or Rembrandt? Is it the same power that makes his heart leap at the sight of one woman and not another? Does *Homage to the Spanish Republic* correspond to some indwelling shape in his soul? What of the woman who is to be his fate? Is her shadow already stored in his inner darkness? How much longer before she reveals herself? When she does, will he be prepared?

What the answer is he cannot say. But if he can meet her as an equal, her, the Destined One, then their lovemaking will be unexampled, that he is sure of, an ecstasy bordering on death; and when he returns to life afterwards it will be as a new being, transformed. A flash of extinction like the touching of opposite poles, like the mating of twins; then the slow rebirth. He must be ready for it. Readiness is all.

At the Everyman Cinema there is a season of Satyajit Ray. He watches the Apu trilogy on successive nights in a state of rapt absorption. In Apu's bitter, trapped mother, his engaging, feckless father he recognizes, with a pang of guilt, his own parents. But it is the music above all that grips him, dizzyingly complex interplays between drums and stringed instruments, long arias on the flute whose scale or mode – he does not know enough about music theory to be sure which – catches at his heart, sending him into a mood of sensual melancholy that lasts long after the film has ended.

Hitherto he has found in Western music, in Bach above all, everything he needs. Now he encounters something that is not in Bach, though there are intimations of it: a joyous yielding of the reasoning, comprehending mind to the dance of the fingers.

He hunts through record shops, and in one of them finds an LP of a sitar player named Ustad Vilayat Khan, with his brother – a younger brother, to judge from the picture – on the veena, and an unnamed tabla player. He does not have a gramophone of his own, but he is able to listen to the first ten minutes in the shop. It is all there: the hovering exploration of tone-sequences, the quivering emotion, the ecstatic rushes. He cannot believe his good fortune. A new continent, and all for a mere nine shillings! He takes the record back to his room, packs it away between sleeves of cardboard till the day when he will be able to listen to it again.

There is an Indian couple living in the room below him. They have a baby that sometimes, faintly, cries. He exchanges nods with the man when they pass on the stairs. The woman rarely emerges.

One evening there is a knock at his door. It is the Indian. Would he like to have a meal with them the next evening?

He accepts, but with misgivings. He is not used to strong spices. Will he be able to eat without spluttering and making a fool of himself?

When he arrives, he is at once put at his ease. The family is from South India; they are vegetarians. Hot spices are not an essential part of Indian cuisine, explains his host: they were introduced only to hide the taste of rotting meat. South Indian food is quite gentle on the palate. And indeed, so it proves to be. What is set before him – coconut soup spiced with cardamom and cloves, an omelette – is positively milky.

His host is an engineer. He and his wife have been in England for several years. They are happy here, he says. Their present accommodation is the best they have had thus far. The room is spacious, the house quiet and orderly. Of course they are not fond of the English climate. But – he shrugs his shoulders – one must take the rough with the smooth.

His wife barely enters the conversation. She serves them without herself eating, then retires to the corner where the baby lies in his cot. Her English is not good, her husband says.

His engineer neighbour admires Western science and technology, complains that India is backward. Though paeans to machines usually bore him, he says nothing to contradict the man. These are the first people in England to invite him into their home. More than that: they are people of colour, they are aware he is South African, yet they have extended a hand to him. He is grateful.

The question is, what should he do with his gratitude? It is inconceivable that he should invite them, husband and wife and no doubt crying baby, to his room on the top floor to eat packet soup followed by, if not chipolatas, then macaroni in cheese sauce. But how else does one return hospitality?

A week passes and he does nothing, then a second week. He feels more and more embarrassed. He begins listening at his door in the mornings, waiting for the engineer to leave for work before he steps out on to the landing.

There must be some gesture to make, some simple act of reciprocation, but he cannot find it, or else will not, and it is fast becoming too late anyway. What is wrong with him? Why does he make the most ordinary things so hard for himself? If the answer is that it is his nature, what is the good of having a nature like that? Why not change his nature?

But is it his nature? He doubts that. It does not feel like nature, it feels like a sickness, a moral sickness: meanness, poverty of spirit, no different in its essence from his coldness with women. Can one make art out of a sickness like that? And if one can, what does that say about art?

On a noticeboard outside a Hampstead newsagent's he reads an advertisement: 'Fourth required for flat in Swiss Cottage. Own room, share kitchen.'

He does not like sharing. He prefers living on his own. But as long as he lives on his own he will never break out of his isolation. He telephones, makes an appointment.

The man who shows him the flat is a few years older than he. He is bearded, wears a blue Nehru jacket with gold buttons down the front. His name is Miklos, and he is from Hungary. The flat itself is clean and airy; the room that will be his is larger than the room he rents at present, more modern too. 'I'll take it,' he tells Miklos without hesitation. 'Shall I give you a deposit?'

But it is not as simple as that. 'Leave your name and number and I'll put you on the list,' says Miklos.

For three days he waits. On the fourth day he telephones. Miklos is not in, says the girl who answers. The room? Oh, the room is gone, it went days ago.

Her voice has a faint foreign huskiness to it; no doubt she is beautiful, intelligent, sophisticated. He does not ask whether she is Hungarian. But if he had got the room, he would now be sharing a flat with her. Who is she? What is her name? Was she his destined love, and has his destiny now escaped him? Who is the fortunate one who has been granted the room and the future that should have been his?

He had the impression, when he called at the flat, that Miklos was showing him around rather perfunctorily. He can only think that Miklos was looking for someone who would bring more to the economy of the household than just a quarter of the rent, someone who would offer gaiety or style or romance as well. Summing him up in a glance, Miklos found him lacking in gaiety, style and romance, and rejected him.

He should have taken the initiative. 'I am not what I may seem to be,' he should have said. 'I may look like a clerk, but in reality I am a poet, or a poet to be. Furthermore, I will pay my share of the rent punctiliously, which is more than most poets will do.' But he had not spoken up, had not pleaded, however abjectly, for himself and his vocation; and now it is too late.

How does a Hungarian come to dispose over a flat in fashionable Swiss Cottage, to dress in the latest mode, to wake up

96

in the lazy late morning with the no doubt beautiful girl with the husky voice beside him in bed, while he has to slave the day away for IBM and live in a dreary room off the Archway Road? How have the keys that unlock the pleasures of London come into the possession of Miklos? Where do such people find the money to support their life of ease?

He has never liked people who disobey the rules. If the rules are ignored, life ceases to make sense: one might as well, like Ivan Karamazov, hand back one's ticket and retire. Yet London seems to be full of people who ignore the rules and get away with it. He seems to be the only one stupid enough to play by the rules, he and the other dark-suited, bespectacled, harried clerks he sees in the trains. What, then, should he do? Should he follow Ivan? Should he follow Miklos? Whichever he follows, it seems to him, he loses. For he has no talent for lying or deception or rule-bending, just as he has no talent for pleasure or fancy clothes. His sole talent is for misery, dull, honest misery. If this city offers no reward for misery, what is he doing here?

TWELVE

EACH WEEK A letter arrives from his mother, a pale blue aero-gramme addressed in neat block capitals. It is with exasperation that he receives these evidences of her unchanging love for him. Will his mother not understand that when he departed Cape Town he cut all bonds with the past? How can he make her accept that the process of turning himself into a different person that began when he was fifteen will be carried through remorse-lessly until all memory of the family and the country he left behind is extinguished? When will she see that he has grown so far away from her that he might as well be a stranger?

In her letters his mother tells him family news, tells him of her latest work assignments (she moves from school to school substituting for teachers away on sick leave). She ends her letters hoping that his health is good, that he is taking care to wear warm clothes, that he has not succumbed to the influenza she has heard to be sweeping across Europe. As for South African affairs, she does not write about those because he has made it plain he is not interested.

He mentions that he has mislaid his gloves on a train. A mistake. Promptly a package arrives by air mail: a pair of sheep-skin mittens. The stamps cost more than the mittens.

She writes her letters on Sunday evenings and posts them in

time for the Monday-morning collection. He can imagine the scene all too easily, in the flat into which she and his father and his brother moved when they had to sell the house in Rondebosch. Supper is over. She clears the table, dons her glasses, draws the lamp nearer. 'What are you doing now?' asks his father, who dreads Sunday evenings, when the *Argus* has been read from end to end and there is nothing left to do. 'I must write to John,' she replies, pursing her lips, shutting him out. *Dearest John,* she begins.

What does she hope to achieve by her letters, this obstinate, graceless woman? Can she not recognize that proofs of her fidelity, no matter how dogged, will never make him relent and come back? Can she not accept that he is not normal? She should concentrate her love on his brother and forget him. His brother is a simpler and more innocent being. His brother has a soft heart. Let his brother take on the burden of loving her; let his brother be told that from now on he is her firstborn, her best beloved. Then he, the new-forgotten one, will be free to make his own life.

She writes every week but he does not write every week in return. That would be too much like reciprocation. Only now and then does he reply, and his letters are brief, saying little except that, by the fact of their having been written, he must still be in the land of the living.

That is the worst of it. That is the trap she has built, a trap he has not yet found a way out of. If he were to cut all ties, if he were not to write at all, she would draw the worst conclusion, the worst possible; and the very thought of the grief that would pierce her at that moment makes him want to block his ears and eyes. As long as she is alive he dare not die. As long as she is alive, therefore, his life is not his own. He may not be reckless with it. Though he does not particularly love himself, he must, for her sake, take care of himself, to the point even of dressing warmly, eating the right food, taking vitamin C. As for suicide, of that there can be no question.

What news he gets about South Africa comes from the BBC and the *Manchester Guardian*. He reads the *Guardian* reports with dread. A farmer ties one of his workers to a tree and flogs him to death. Police fire at random into a crowd. A prisoner is found dead in his cell, hanging from a strip of blanket, his face bruised and bloody. Horror upon horror, atrocity upon atrocity, without relief.

He knows his mother's opinions. She thinks South Africa is misunderstood by the world. Blacks in South Africa are better off than anywhere else in Africa. The strikes and protests are fomented by communist agitators. As for the farm labourers who are paid their wages in the form of mealie-meal and have to dress their children in jute bags against the winter cold, his mother concedes that that is a disgrace. But such things happen only in the Transvaal. It is the Afrikaners of the Transvaal, with their sullen hatreds and their hard hearts, who give the country such a bad name.

His own opinion, which he does not hesitate to communicate to her, is that, instead of making speech after speech at the United Nations, the Russians ought to invade South Africa without delay. They should land paratroops in Pretoria, take Verwoerd and his cronies captive, line them up against a wall, and shoot them.

What the Russians should do next, after shooting Verwoerd, he does not say, not having thought it out. Justice must be done, that is all that matters; the rest is politics, and he is not interested in politics. As far back as he can remember, Afrikaners have trampled on people because, they claim, they were once trampled upon. Well, let the wheel turn again, let force be replied to with greater force. He is glad to be out of it.

South Africa is like an albatross around his neck. He wants it removed, he does not care how, so that he can begin to breathe.

He does not have to buy the *Manchester Guardian*. There are other, easier newspapers: *The Times*, for instance, or the *Daily Telegraph*. But the *Manchester Guardian* can be relied on not to miss anything from South Africa that will make the soul cringe within him. Reading the *Manchester Guardian*, he can at least be sure he knows the worst.

He has not contacted Astrid for weeks. Now she telephones. Her time in England is up, she is going home to Austria. 'I guess I won't see you again,' she says, 'so I called to say goodbye.'

She is trying to be matter-of-fact, but he can hear the tearfulness in her voice. Guiltily he proposes a meeting. They have coffee together; she comes back to his room and spends the night ('our last night,' she calls it), clinging to him, crying softly. Early the next morning (it is a Sunday) he hears her creep out of bed and tiptoe to the bathroom on the landing to get dressed. When she comes back he pretends to be asleep. He has only to give the slightest signal, he knows, and she will stay. If there are things he would prefer to do first, before paying attention to her, like reading the newspaper, she will sit quietly in a corner and wait. That seems to be how girls are taught to behave in Klagenfurt: to demand nothing, to wait until the man is ready, and then to serve him.

He would like to be nicer to Astrid, so young, so alone in the big city. He would like to dry her tears, make her smile; he would like to prove to her that his heart is not as hard as it seems, that he is capable of responding to her willingness with a willingness of his own, a willingness to cuddle her as she wants to be cuddled and give ear to her stories about her mother and brothers back home. But he must be careful. Too much warmth and she might cancel her ticket, stay in London, move in with him. Two of the defeated sheltering in each other's arms, consoling each other: the prospect is too humiliating. They might as well get married, he and Astrid, then spend the rest of their lives looking after each other like invalids. So he gives no signal, but lies with his eyelids clenched till he hears the creak of the stairs and the click of the front door.

It is December, and the weather has turned bitter. Snow falls, the snow turns to slush, the slush freezes: on the sidewalks one has to pick one's way from foothold to foothold like a mountaineer. A blanket of fog enfolds the city, fog thick with coal dust and sulphur. The electricity fails; trains stop running; old people freeze to death in their homes. The worst winter of the century, say the newspapers.

He tramps up Archway Road, slipping and sliding on the ice, holding a scarf over his face, trying not to breathe. His clothes smell of sulphur, there is a foul taste in his mouth, when he coughs he coughs up black phlegm. In South Africa it is summer. If he were there he could be on Strandfontein beach, running over mile after mile of white sand under a great blue sky.

During the night a pipe bursts in his room. The floor is flooded. He wakes up surrounded by a sheet of ice.

It is like the blitz all over again, say the newspapers. They print stories of soup kitchens for the homeless run by women's auxiliaries, of repair crews toiling through the night. The crisis is bringing out the best in Londoners, they say, who confront adversity with quiet strength and a ready quip.

As for him, he may dress like a Londoner, tramp to work like a Londoner, suffer the cold like a Londoner, but he has no ready quips. Not in a month of Sundays would Londoners take him for the real thing. On the contrary, Londoners recognize him at once as another of those foreigners who for daft reasons of their own choose to live where they don't belong.

How long will he have to live in England before it is allowed that he has become the real thing, become English? Will getting a British passport be enough, or does an odd-sounding foreign name mean he will be shut out for ever? And 'becoming English' – what does that mean anyhow? England is the home of two nations: he will have to choose between them, choose whether to be middle-class English or working-class English. Already he seems to have chosen. He wears the uniform of the middle class, reads a middle-class newspaper, imitates middle-class speech. But mere externals such as those are not going to be enough to get him admission, not by a long chalk. Admission to the middle class – full admission, not a temporary ticket valid for certain times of the day on certain days of the year – was decided, as far as he can tell, years ago, even generations ago, according to rules that will forever be dark to him.

As for the working class, he does not share its recreations, can barely understand its speech, has never felt the slightest motion of welcome from it. The girls at IBM have their own working-class boyfriends, are wrapped up in thoughts of marriage and babies and council houses, respond frostily to overtures. He may be living in England, but it is certainly not by invitation of the English working class.

There are other South Africans in London, thousands of them, if he is to believe report. There are Canadians too, Australians, New Zealanders, even Americans. But these people are not immigrants, are not here to settle, to become English. They have come to have fun or to study or to earn some money before going on a tour of Europe. When they have had enough of the Old World they will go home and take up their real lives.

There are Europeans in London as well, not only language

students but refugees from the Eastern Bloc and, further back, from Nazi Germany. But their situation is different from his. He is not a refugee; or rather, a claim on his part to be a refugee will get him nowhere with the Home Office. Who is oppressing you, the Home Office will say? From what are you fleeing? From boredom, he will reply. From philistinism. From atrophy of the moral life. From shame. Where will such a plea get him?

Then there is Paddington. He walks along Maida Vale or Kilburn High Road at six o'clock in the evening and sees, under the ghostly sodium lights, throngs of West Indians trudging back to their lodgings, muffled against the cold. Their shoulders are bowed, their hands are thrust deep in their pockets, their skins have a greyish, powdery hue. What draws them from Jamaica and Trinidad to this heartless city where the cold seeps up from the very stones of the streets, where the hours of daylight are spent in drudgery and the evenings huddled over a gas fire in a hired room with peeling walls and sagging furniture? Surely they are not all here to find fame as poets.

The people he works with are too polite to express their opinion of foreigner visitors. Nevertheless, from certain of their silences he knows he is not wanted in their country, not positively wanted. On the subject of West Indians they are silent too, but he can read the signs. NIGGER GO HOME say slogans painted on walls. NO COLOURED say notices in the windows of lodging-houses. Month by month the government tightens its immigration laws. West Indians are halted at the dockside in Liverpool, detained until they grow desperate, then shipped back to where they came from. If he is not made to feel as nakedly unwelcome as they are, it can only be because of his protective coloration: his Moss Brothers suit, his pale skin.

THIRTEEN

'AFTER CAREFUL CONSIDERATION I have reached the conclusion . . . ' 'After much soul-searching I have come to the conclusion . . .'

He has been in the service of IBM for over a year: winter, spring, summer, autumn, another winter, and now the beginning of another spring. Even inside the Newman Street bureau, a boxlike building with sealed windows, he can feel the suave change in the air. He cannot go on like this. He cannot sacrifice any more of his life to the principle that human beings should have to labour in misery for their bread, a principle he seems to adhere to though he has no idea where he picked it up. He cannot forever be demonstrating to his mother in Cape Town that he has made a solid life for himself and therefore that she can stop worrying about him. Usually he does not know his own mind, does not care to know his own mind. To know one's own mind too well spells, in his view, the death of the creative spark. But in this case he cannot afford to drift on in his usual haze of indecision. He must leave IBM. He must get out, no matter how much it will cost in humiliation.

Over the past year his handwriting has, beyond his control, been growing smaller, smaller and more secretive. Now, sitting at his desk, writing what will be the announcement of his resignation, he tries consciously to make the letters larger, the loops fatter and more confident-seeming.

'After lengthy reflection,' he writes at last, 'I have reached the conclusion that my future does not lie with IBM. In terms of my contract I therefore wish to tender one month's notice.'

He signs the letter, seals it, addresses it to Dr B. L. McIver, Manager, Programming Division, and drops it discreetly in the tray marked INTERNAL. No one in the office gives him a glance. He takes his seat again.

Until three o'clock, when the mail is next collected, there is time for second thoughts, time to slip the letter out of the tray and tear it up. Once the letter is delivered, however, the die will be cast. By tomorrow the news will have spread through the building: one of McIver's people, one of the programmers on the second floor, the South African, has resigned. No one will want to be seen speaking to him. He will be sent to Coventry. That is how it is at IBM. No false sentiment. He will be marked as a quitter, a loser, unclean.

At three o'clock the woman comes around for the mail. He bends over his papers, his heart thumping.

Half an hour later he is summoned to McIver's office. McIver is in a cold fury. 'What is this?' he says, indicating the letter that lies open on the desk.

'I have decided to resign.'

'Why?'

He had guessed McIver would take it badly. McIver is the one who interviewed him for the job, who accepted and approved him, who swallowed the story that he was just an ordinary bloke from the colonies planning a career in computers. McIver has his own bosses, to whom he will have to explain his mistake.

McIver is a tall man. He dresses sleekly, speaks with an Oxford accent. He has no interest in programming as a science or skill or craft or whatever it is. He is simply a manager. That is what he is good at: allotting tasks to people, managing their time, driving them, getting his money's worth out of them.

'Why?' says McIver again, impatiently.

'I don't find working for IBM very satisfying at a human level. I don't find it fulfilling.'

'Go on.'

'I was hoping for something more.'

'And what may that be?'

'I was hoping for friendships.'

'You find the atmosphere unfriendly?'

'No, not unfriendly, not at all. People have been very kind. But being friendly is not the same thing as friendship.'

He had hoped the letter would be allowed to be his last word. But that hope was naïve. He should have realized they would take it as nothing but the first shot in a war.

'What else? If there is something else on your mind, this is your chance to bring it out.'

'Nothing else.'

'Nothing else. I see. You are missing friendships. You haven't found friends.'

'Yes, that's right. I'm not blaming anyone. The fault is probably my own.'

'And for that you want to resign.'

'Yes.'

Now that the words are out they sound stupid, and they are stupid. He is being manoeuvred into saying stupid things. But he should have expected that. That is how they will make him pay for rejecting them and the job they have given him, a job with IBM, the market leader. Like a beginner in chess, pushed into corners and mated in ten moves, in eight moves, in seven moves. A lesson in domination. Well, let them do it. Let them play their moves, and let him play his stupid, easily foreseen, easily forestalled return moves, until they are bored with the game and let him go.

With a brusque gesture McIver terminates the interview. That, for the moment, is that. He is free to return to his desk. For once there is not even the obligation to work late. He can leave the building at five, win the evening for himself.

The next morning, through McIver's secretary – McIver himself sweeps past him, not returning his greeting – he is instructed to report without delay to IBM Head Office in the City, to the Personnel Department.

The man in Personnel who hears his case has clearly had recounted to him the complaint about the friendships IBM has failed to supply. A folder lies open on the desk before him; as the interrogation proceeds, he ticks off points. How long has he been unhappy in his work? Did he at any stage discuss his unhappiness with his superior? If not, why not? Have his colleagues at Newman Street been positively unfriendly? No? Then would he expand on his complaint?

The more often the words *friend, friendship, friendly* are spoken, the odder they sound. If you are looking for friends, he can imagine the man saying, join a club, play skittles, fly model planes, collect stamps. Why expect your employer, IBM, International Business Machines, manufacturer of electronic calculators and computers, to provide them for you?

And of course the man is right. What right has he to complain, in this country above all, where everyone is so cool to everyone else? Is that not what he admires the English for: their emotional restraint? Is that not why he is writing, in his spare time, a thesis on the works of Ford Madox Ford, half-German celebrator of English laconism?

Confused and stumbling, he expands on his complaint. His expansion is as obscure to the Personnel man as the complaint

108

itself. *Misapprehension*: that is the word the man is hunting for. *Employee was under a misapprehension*: that would be an appropriate formulation. But he does not feel like being helpful. Let them find their own way of pigeonholing him.

What the man is particularly keen to find out is what he will do next. Is his talk about lack of friendship merely a cover for a move from IBM to one of IBM's competitors in the field of business machines? Have promises been made to him, have inducements been offered?

He could not be more earnest in his denials. He does not have another job lined up, with a rival or anyone else. He has not been interviewed. He is leaving IBM simply to get out of IBM. He wants to be free, that is all.

The more he talks, the sillier he sounds, the more out of place in the world of business. But at least he is not saying, 'I am leaving IBM in order to become a poet.' That secret, at least, is still his own.

Out of the blue, in the midst of all this, comes a phone call from Caroline. She is on vacation on the south coast, in Bognor Regis, and at a loose end. Why does he not catch a train and spend Saturday with her?

She meets him at the station. From a shop on the Main Street they hire bicycles; soon they are cycling along empty country lanes amid fields of young wheat. It is unseasonably warm. Sweat pours from him. His clothes are wrong for the occasion: grey flannels, a jacket. Caroline wears a brief tomato-coloured tunic and sandals. Her blonde hair flashes, her long legs gleam as she turns the pedals; she looks like a goddess.

What is she doing in Bognor Regis, he asks? Staying with an aunt, she replies, a long-lost English aunt. He does not inquire further.

They stop at the roadside, cross a fence. Caroline has brought sandwiches; they find a spot in the shade of a chestnut tree and have their picnic. Afterwards, he senses she would not mind if he made love to her. But he is nervous, out here in the open where at any moment a farmer or even a constable might descend on them and demand to know what they think they are up to.

'I've resigned from IBM,' he says.

'That's good. What will you do next?'

'I don't know. I'll just drift for a while, I think.'

She waits to hear more, waits to hear his plans. But he has no more to offer, no plans, no ideas. What a dullard he is! Why does a girl like Caroline bother to keep him in tow, a girl who has acclimatized to England, made a success of her life, left him behind in every way? Only one explanation occurs to him: that she still sees him as he was in Cape Town, when he could still present himself as a poet to be, when he was not yet what he has become, what IBM has made of him: a eunuch, a drone, a worried boy hurrying to catch the 8.17 to the office.

Elsewhere in Britain, employees who resign are given a sendoff – if not a gold watch then at least a get-together during the tea break, a speech, a round of applause and good wishes, whether sincere or insincere. He has been in the country long enough to know that. But not at IBM. IBM is not Britain. IBM is the new wave, the new way. That is why IBM is going to cut a swathe through the British opposition. The opposition is still caught up in old, slack, inefficient British ways. IBM, on the contrary, is lean and hard and merciless. So there is no sendoff for him on his last day at work. He clears his desk in silence, says his goodbyes to his programmer colleagues. 'What will you be doing?' asks one of them cautiously. All have clearly heard the friendship story; it makes them stiff and uncomfortable. 'Oh, I'll see what comes up,' he replies.

It is an interesting feeling, waking up the next morning with nowhere in particular to go. A sunny day: he catches a train to Leicester Square, does a tour of the bookshops on Charing Cross Road. He has a day's growth of stubble; he has decided to wear a beard. With a beard he will perhaps not look so out of place among the elegant young men and beautiful girls who pour out of the language schools and ride the Underground. Then let chance take its course.

From now on, he has decided, he will put himself in chance's way at every turn. Novels are full of chance meetings that lead to romance – romance or tragedy. He is ready for romance, ready even for tragedy, ready for anything, in fact, so long as he will be consumed by it and remade. That is why he is in London, after all: to be rid of his old self and revealed in his new, true, passionate self; and now there is no impediment to his quest.

The days pass and he simply does as he wishes. Technically speaking, his position is illegal. Clipped to his passport is the work permit that allows him to reside in Britain. Now that he has no work, the permit has lost its power. But if he lies low, perhaps they – the authorities, the police, whoever is responsible – will overlook him.

Ahead on the horizon looms the problem of money. His savings will not last indefinitely. He has nothing worth selling. Prudently he gives up buying books; he walks, when the weather is good, rather than catching trains; he lives on bread and cheese and apples.

Chance does not bestow any of her blessings on him. But chance is unpredictable, one must give chance time. For the day when chance will at last smile on him he can only wait in readiness.

FOURTEEN

WITH FREEDOM TO do as he pleases, he has soon read to the end of the sprawling corpus of Ford's writings. The time is nigh for him to deliver his judgment. What will he say? In the sciences one is permitted to report negative results, failures to confirm hypotheses. How about the arts? If he has nothing new to say about Ford, would the correct, the honourable action be to confess he has made a mistake, resign his studentship, return his bursary; or, in place of a thesis, would it be permissible to turn in a report on what a let-down his subject has been, how disappointed he is in his hero?

Briefcase in hand, he strolls out of the British Museum and joins the crowd passing down Great Russell Street: thousands of souls, not one of whom cares a fig what he thinks of Ford Madox Ford or anything else. When he first arrived in London he used to stare boldly into the faces of these passers-by, searching out the unique essence of each. *Look, I am looking at you!* he was saying. But bold stares got him nowhere in a city where, he soon discovered, neither men nor women met his gaze but, on the contrary, coolly evaded it.

Each refusal of his gaze felt like a tiny knife-prick. Again and again he was being noted, found wanting, turned down. Soon he began to lose his nerve, to flinch even before the refusal came. With women he found it easier to look covertly, steal looks. That, it would seem, was how looking was done in London. But in stolen looks there was – he could not rid himself of the feeling – something shifty, unclean. Preferable not to look at all. Preferable to be incurious about one's neighbours, indifferent.

In the time he has been here he has changed a great deal; he is not sure it is for the better. During the winter just past there were times when he thought he would die of cold and misery and loneliness. But he has pulled through, after a fashion. By the time the next winter arrives, cold and misery will have less purchase on him. Then he will be on his way to becoming a proper Londoner, hard as stone. Turning to stone was not one of his aims, but it may be what he will have to settle for.

All in all, London is proving to be a great chastener. Already his ambitions are more modest than they used to be, much more modest. Londoners disappointed him, at first, with the poverty of their ambitions. Now he is on his way to joining them. Each day the city chastens him, chastises him; like a beaten dog, he is learning.

Not knowing what, if anything, he wants to say about Ford, he lies abed later and later in the mornings. When finally he sits down at his desk he is unable to concentrate. Summertime contributes to his confusion. The London he knows is a city of winter where one plods through each day with nothing to look forward to but nightfall and bedtime and oblivion. Through these balmy summer days, which seem made for ease and pleasure, the testing continues: what part is being tested he is no longer sure. Sometimes it seems he is being tested simply for testing's sake, to see whether he will endure the test.

About quitting IBM he has no regrets. But now he has no one at all to speak to, not even Bill Briggs. Day after day goes

113

by when not a word passes his lips. He begins to mark them off with an *S* in his diary: days of silence.

Outside the Underground station he bumps by mistake against a little old man selling newspapers. 'Sorry!' he says. 'Watch where you're going!' snarls the man. 'Sorry!' he repeats.

Sorry: the word comes heavily out of his mouth, like a stone. Does a single word of indeterminate class count as speech? Has what has occurred between himself and the old man been an instance of human contact, or is it better described as mere social interaction, like the touching of feelers between ants? To the old man, certainly, it was nothing. All day long the old man stands there with his stack of papers, muttering angrily to himself; he is always waiting for a chance to abuse some passer-by. Whereas in his own case the memory of that single word will persist for weeks, perhaps for the rest of his life. Bumping into people, saying 'Sorry!', getting abused: a ruse, a cheap way of forcing a conversation. How to trick loneliness.

He is in the vale of testing and not doing very well. Yet he cannot be the only one to be tested. There must be people who have passed through the vale and come out on the other side; there must be people who have dodged the testing entirely. He too could dodge the test if he preferred. He could run away to Cape Town, for instance, and never come back. But is that what he wants to do? Surely not, not yet.

Yet what if he stays on and fails the test, fails disgracefully? What if, alone in his room, he begins to cry and cannot cease? What if one morning he finds that he lacks the courage to get up, finds it easier to spend the day in bed – that day and the next, and the next, in sheets that get grubbier and grubbier? What happens to people like that, people who cannot stand up to the testing, and crack?

He knows the answer. They are shipped off somewhere to be

taken care of – to some hospital, home, institution. In his case he will be simply be shipped back to South Africa. The English have enough of their own to take care of, enough people who fail the testing. Why should they take care of foreigners too?

He hovers before a doorway in Greek Street, Soho. *Jackie – Model*, says the card above the bell. He is in need of human intercourse: what could be more human than sexual intercourse? Artists have frequented prostitutes since time immemorial and are none the worse for it, that he knows from his reading. In fact, artists and prostitutes are on the same side of the social battle-lines. But *Jackie – Model*: is a model in this country always a prostitute, or in the business of selling oneself are there gradations, gradations no one has told him about? Might *model* in Greek Street stand for something quite specialized, for specialized tastes: a woman posing naked under a light, for instance, with men in raincoats standing around in the shadows, gazing shiftily at her, leering? Once he has rung the bell, will there be a way of inquiring, finding out what is what, before he is entirely sucked in? What if Jackie herself turns out to be old or fat or ugly? And what of the etiquette? Is this how one visits someone like Jackie – unannounced – or is one expected to telephone beforehand and make an appointment? How much does one pay? Is there a scale that every man in London knows, every man except him? What if he is identified at once as a hick, a dummy, and overcharged?

He falters, retreats.

In the street a man in a dark suit passes by who seems to recognize him, seems about to stop and speak. It is one of the senior programmers from the IBM days, someone he did not have much contact with, but always thought well disposed toward him. He hesitates, then with an embarrassed nod hurries past.

'So what are you doing with yourself these days – leading a

life of pleasure?' – that is what the man would say, smiling genially. What could he say in return? That we cannot always be working, that life is short, we must taste its pleasures while we can? What a joke, and what a scandal too! For the stubborn, mean lives that his ancestors lived, sweating in their dark clothes in the heat and dust of the Karoo, to eventuate in this: a young man sauntering around a foreign city, eating up his savings, whoring, pretending to be an artist! How can he so casually betray them and then hope to escape their avenging ghosts? It was not in the nature of those men and women to be gay and have pleasure, and it is not in his. He is their child, foredoomed from birth to be gloomy and suffer. How else does poetry come anyway, except out of suffering, like blood squeezed from a stone?

South Africa is a wound within him. How much longer before the wound stops bleeding? How much longer will he have to grit his teeth and endure before he is able to say, 'Once upon a time I used to live in South Africa but now I live in England'?

Now and again, for an instant, it is given to him to see himself from the outside: a whispering, worried boy-man, so dull and ordinary that you would not spare him a second glance. These flashes of illumination disturb him; rather than holding on to them, he tries to bury them in darkness, forget them. Is the self he sees at such moments merely what he appears to be, or is it what he really is? What if Oscar Wilde is right, and there is no deeper truth than appearance? Is it possible to be dull and ordinary not only on the surface but to one's deepest depths, and yet be an artist? Might T. S. Eliot, for instance, be secretly dull to his depths, and might Eliot's claim that the artist's personality is irrelevant to his work be nothing but a stratagem to conceal his own dullness?

Perhaps; but he does not believe it. If it comes down to a

choice between believing Wilde and believing Eliot, he will always believe Eliot. If Eliot chooses to seem dull, chooses to wear a suit and work in a bank and call himself J. Alfred Prufrock, it must be as a disguise, as part of the necessary cunning of the artist in the modern age.

Sometimes, as a relief from walking the city streets, he retreats to Hampstead Heath. There the air is gently warm, the paths full of young mothers pushing prams or chatting to each other as their children gambol. Such peace and contentment! He used to be impatient of poems about budding flowers and zephyrous breezes. Now, in the land where those poems were written, he begins to understand how deep gladness can run at the return of the sun.

Tired out, one Sunday afternoon, he folds his jacket into a pillow, stretches out on the greensward, and sinks into a sleep or half-sleep in which consciousness does not vanish but continues to hover. It is a state he has not known before: in his very blood he seems to feel the steady wheeling of the earth. The faraway cries of children, the birdsong, the whirr of insects gather force and come together in a paean of joy. His heart swells. *At last!* he thinks. At last it has come, the moment of ecstatic unity with the All! Fearful that the moment will slip away, he tries to put a halt to the clatter of thought, tries simply to be a conduit for the great universal force that has no name.

It lasts no more than seconds in clock time, this signal event. But when he gets up and dusts off his jacket, he is refreshed, renewed. He journeyed to the great dark city to be tested and transformed, and here, on this patch of green under the mild spring sun, word of his progress has, surprisingly, come. If he has not utterly been transfigured, then at least he has been blessed with a hint that he belongs on this earth.

FIFTEEN

HE MUST FIND ways to save money. Lodging is his single biggest expense. He advertises in the classified section of the Hampstead local paper: 'House-sitter available, responsible professional man, long or short term.' To the two callers who respond he gives IBM as his work address and hopes they will not check up. The impression he tries to create is of rigid propriety. The act works well enough for him to be engaged to look after a flat in Swiss Cottage for the month of June.

He will not, alas, have the flat to himself. The flat belongs to a divorced woman with a small daughter. While she is away in Greece, the child and the child's nanny will be in his care. His duties will be simple: to attend to the mail, pay the bills, be at hand in case of emergencies. He will have one room as his own, and access to the kitchen.

There is also an ex-husband in the picture. The ex-husband will appear on Sundays to take his daughter out. He is, as his employer or patroness puts it, 'a bit hot-tempered,' and should not be allowed to 'get away with anything.' What exactly might the husband want to get away with, he inquires? Keeping the child overnight, he is told. Sniffing through the flat. Taking things. On no account, no matter what story he spins – she gives him a meaningful look – should he be allowed to take things.

So he begins to understand why he is needed. The nanny, who comes from Malawi, no great distance from South Africa, is perfectly capable of cleaning the flat, doing the shopping, feeding the child, walking her to and from kindergarten. She is perhaps even capable of paying the bills. What she is not capable of is standing up to the man who until recently was her employer and whom she still refers to as *the master*. The job he has let himself in for is in fact that of a guard, guarding the flat and its contents from the man who until recently used to live here.

On the first day of June he hires a taxi and moves, with his trunk and suitcase, from the seedy surroundings of Archway Road to the discreet elegance of Hampstead.

The flat is large and airy; sunlight streams in through the windows; there are soft white carpets, bookcases full of promising-looking books. It is quite unlike what he has seen thus far in London. He cannot believe his luck.

While he unpacks, the little girl, his new charge, stands at the door of his room watching his every movement. He has never had to look after a child before. Does he, because he is in a sense young, have a natural bond with children? Slowly, gently, wearing his most reassuring smile, he closes the door on her. After a moment she pushes it open and gravely continues to inspect him. *My house*, she seems to be saying. *What are you doing in my house?*

Her name is Fiona. She is five years old. Later in the day he makes an effort to befriend her. In the living room, where she is playing, he gets down on his knees and strokes the cat, a huge, sluggish, neutered male. The cat tolerates the stroking as, it would appear, it tolerates all attentions.

'Does the kitty want his milk?' he asks. 'Shall we get the kitty some milk?'

The child does not stir, does not appear to hear him.

He goes to the fridge, pours milk into the cat's bowl, brings the bowl back, and sets it before the cat. The cat sniffs at the cold milk but does not drink.

The child is winding cord around her dolls, stuffing them into a laundry bag, pulling them out again. If it is a game, it is a game whose meaning he cannot fathom.

'What are your dolls' names?' he asks.

She does not reply.

'What is the golliwog's name? Is it Golly?'

'He's not a golliwog,' says the child.

He gives up. 'I have work to do now,' he says, and retires.

He has been told to call the nanny Theodora. Theodora has yet to reveal her name for him: certainly not *the master*. She occupies a room at the end of the corridor, next to the child's. It is understood that these two rooms and the laundry room are her province. The living room is neutral territory.

Theodora is, he would guess, in her forties. She has been in the Merringtons' service since their last spell in Malawi. The hot-tempered ex-husband is an anthropologist; the Merringtons were in Theodora's country on a field trip, making recordings of tribal music and collecting instruments. Theodora soon became, in Mrs Merrington's words, 'not just a house-help but a friend.' She was brought back to London because of the bond she had forged with the child. Each month she sends home the wages that keep her own children fed and clothed and in school.

And now, all of a sudden, a stranger half this treasure's age has been put in charge of her domain. By her bearing, by her silences, Theodora gives him to understand that she resents his presence.

He does not blame her. The question is, is there more under-lying her resentment than just hurt pride? She must know he is not an Englishman. Does she resent him in his person as a South African, a white, an Afrikaner? She must know what Afrikaners are. There are Afrikaners – big-bellied, red-nosed men in short pants and hats, rolypoly women in shapeless dresses – all over Africa: in Rhodesia, in Angola, in Kenya, certainly in Malawi. Is there anything he can do to make her understand that he is not one of them, that he has quit South Africa, is resolved to put South Africa behind him for ever? *Africa belongs to you, it is yours to do with as you wish*: if he said that to her, out of the blue, across the kitchen table, would she change her mind about him?

Africa is yours. What had seemed perfectly natural while he still called that continent his home seems more and more preposterous from the perspective of Europe: that a handful of Hollanders should have waded ashore on Woodstock beach and claimed ownership of foreign territory they had never laid eyes on before; that their descendants should now regard that territory as theirs by birthright. Doubly absurd, given that the first landing-party misunderstood its orders, or chose to misunderstand them. Its orders were to dig a garden and grow spinach and onions for the East India fleet. Two acres, three acres, five acres at most: that was all that was needed. It was never intended that they should steal the best part of Africa. If they had only obeyed their orders, he would not be here, nor would Theodora. Theodora would happily be pounding millet under Malawian skies and he would be – what? He would be sitting at a desk in an office in rainy Rotterdam, adding up figures in a ledger.

Theodora is a fat woman, fat in every detail, from her chubby cheeks to her swelling ankles. Walking, she rocks from side to side, wheezing from the exertion. Indoors she wears slippers; when she takes the child to school in the mornings she squeezes her feet into tennis shoes, puts on a long black coat and knitted hat. She works six days of the week. On Sundays she goes to church, but otherwise spends her day of rest at home. She never uses the telephone; she appears to have no social circle. What she does when she is by herself he cannot guess. He does not venture into her room or the child's, even when they are out of the flat: in return, he hopes, they will not poke around in his room.

Among the Merringtons' books is a folio of pornographic pictures from imperial China. Men in oddly-shaped hats part their robes and aim grossly distended penises at the genitals of tiny women who obligingly part and raise their legs. The women are pale and soft, like bee-grubs; their puny legs seem merely glued to their abdomens. Do Chinese women still look like that, he wonders, with their clothes off, or has re-education and labour in the fields given them proper bodies, proper legs? What chance is there he will ever find out?

Since he got free lodging by masquerading as a dependable professional man, he has to keep up the pretence of having a job. He gets up early, earlier than he is used to, in order to have breakfast before Theodora and the child begin to stir. Then he shuts himself up in his room. When Theodora returns from taking the child to school, he leaves the flat, ostensibly to go to work. At first he even dons his black suit, but soon relaxes that part of the deception. He comes home at five, sometimes at four.

It is lucky that it is summer, that he is not restricted to the British Museum and the bookshops and cinemas, but can stroll around the public parks. This must have been more or less how his father lived during the long spells when he was out of work: roaming the city in his office clothes or sitting in bars watching the hands of the clock, waiting for a decent hour to go home. Is he after all going to turn out to be his father's son? How deep does it run in him, the strain of fecklessness? Will he turn out to be a drunkard too? Does one need a certain temperament to become a drunkard?

His father's drink was brandy. He tried brandy once, can recollect nothing except an unpleasant, metallic aftertaste. In England people drink beer, whose sourness he dislikes. If he doesn't like liquor, is he safe, inoculated against becoming a drunkard? Are there other, as yet unguessed-at ways in which his father is going to manifest himself in his life?

The ex-husband does not take long to make an appearance. It is Sunday morning, he is dozing in the big, comfortable bed, when suddenly there is a ring at the doorbell and the scrape of a key. He springs out of bed cursing himself. 'Hello, Fiona, Theodora!' comes a voice. There is a scuffling sound, running feet. Then without so much as a knock the door of his room swings open and they are surveying him, the man with the child in his arms. He barely has his trousers on. 'Hello!' says the man, 'what have we here?'

It is one of those expressions the English use – an English policeman, for instance, catching one in a guilty act. Fiona, who could explain what we have here, chooses not to. Instead, from her perch in her father's arms, she looks upon him with undisguised coldness. Her father's daughter: same cool eyes, same brow.

'I'm looking after the flat in Mrs Merrington's absence,' he says.

'Ah yes,' says the man, 'the South African. I had forgotten. Let me introduce myself. Richard Merrington. I used to be lord of the manor here. How are you finding things? Settling in well?'

'Yes, I'm fine.'

'Good.'

Theodora appears with the child's coat and boots. The man lets his daughter slide from his arms. 'And do a wee-wee too,' he tells her, 'before we get in the car.'

Theodora and the child go off. They are left together, he and this handsome, well-dressed man in whose bed he has been sleeping.

'And how long do you plan to be here?' says the man.

'Just till the end of the month.'

'No, I mean how long in this country?'

'Oh, indefinitely. I've left South Africa.'

'Things pretty bad there, are they?'

'Yes.'

'Even for whites?'

How does one respond to a question like that? *If you don't want to perish of shame? If you want to escape the cataclysm to come?* Why do big words sound so out of place in this country?

'Yes,' he says. 'At least I think so.'

'That reminds me,' says the man. He crosses the room to the rack of gramophone records, flips through them, extracting one, two, three.

This is exactly what he was warned against, exactly what he must not allow to happen. 'Excuse me,' he says, 'Mrs Merrington asked me specifically . . .'

The man rises to his full height and faces him. 'Diana asked you what specifically?'

'Not to allow anything to leave the flat.'

'Nonsense. These are my records, she has no use for them.' Coolly he resumes his search, removing more records. 'If you don't believe me, give her a call.'

The child clumps into the room in her heavy boots. 'Ready to go, are we, darling?' says the man. 'Goodbye. I hope all goes well. Goodbye, Theodora. Don't worry, we'll be back before bathtime.' And, bearing his daughter and the records, he is gone.

SIXTEEN

A LETTER ARRIVES from his mother. His brother has bought a car, she writes, an MG that has been in a crash. Instead of studying, his brother is now spending all his time fixing the car, trying to get it to run. He has found new friends too, whom he does not introduce to her. One of them looks Chinese. They all sit around in the garage, smoking; she suspects the friends bring liquor. She is worried. He is on the downward path; how is she to save him?

For his part, he is intrigued. So his brother is at last beginning to free himself from their mother's embrace. Yet what an odd way to choose: automotive mechanics! Does his brother really know how to fix cars? Where did he learn? He had always thought that, of the two, he was better with his hands, more blessed with mechanical sense. Was he wrong about that all the time? What else does his brother have up his sleeve?

There is further news in the letter. His cousin Ilse and a friend will shortly be arriving in England en route to a camping holiday in Switzerland. Will he show them around London? She gives the address of the hostel in Earls Court where they will be staying.

He is astonished that, after all he has said to her, his mother can think that he wants contact with South Africans, and with his father's family in particular. He has not laid eyes on Ilse since they were children. What can he possibly have in common with her, a girl who went to school in the back of nowhere and can think of nothing better to do with a holiday in Europe – a holiday no doubt paid for by her parents – than to tramp around *gemütliche* Switzerland, a country that in all its history has not given birth to one great artist?

Yet now that her name has been mentioned, he cannot put Ilse out of his mind. He remembers her as a rangy, swift-footed child with long blonde hair tied in a pigtail. By now she must be at least eighteen. What will she have turned into? What if all that outdoor living has made of her, for however brief a spell, a beauty? For he has seen the phenomenon many times among farm children: a springtime of physical perfection before the coarsening and thickening commences that will turn them into copies of their parents. Ought he to turn down the chance of walking the streets of London with a tall Aryan huntress at his side?

In his fantasy he recognizes the erotic tingle. What is it about his girl cousins, even the idea of them, that sparks desire in him? Is it simply that they are forbidden? Is that how taboo operates: creating desire by forbidding it? Or is the genesis of his desire less abstract: memories of tussles, girl against boy, body to body, stored since childhood and released now in a rush of sexual feeling? That, perhaps, and the promise of ease, of easiness: two people with a history in common, a country, a family, a blood intimacy from before the first word was spoken. No introductions needed, no fumbling around.

He leaves a message at the Earls Court address. Some days later there is a call: not from Ilse but from the friend, the companion, speaking English clumsily, getting *is* and *are* wrong. She has bad news: Ilse is ill, with flu that has turned into pneumonia.

She is in a nursing home in Bayswater. Their travel plans are held up until she gets better.

He visits Ilse in the nursing home. All his hopes are dashed. She is not a beauty, not even tall, just an ordinary moon-faced girl with mousy hair who wheezes when she talks. He greets her without kissing her, for fear of infection.

The friend is in the room too. Her name is Marianne; she is small and plump; she wears corduroy trousers and boots and exudes good health. For a while they all speak English, then he relents and switches to the language of the family, to Afrikaans. Though it is years since he spoke Afrikaans, he can feel himself relax at once as though sliding into a warm bath.

He had expected to be able to show off his knowledge of London. But the London Ilse and Marianne want to see is not a London he knows. He can tell them nothing about Madame Tussaud's, the Tower, St Paul's, none of which he has visited. He has no idea how one gets to Stratford-on-Avon. What he is able to tell them – which cinemas show foreign films, which bookshops are best for what – they do not care to know.

Ilse is on antibiotics; it will be days before she is herself again. In the meantime Marianne is at a loose end. He suggests a walk along the Thames embankment. In her hiking boots, with her no-nonsense haircut, Marianne from Ficksburg is out of place among the fashionable London girls, but she does not seem to care. Nor does she care if people hear her speaking Afrikaans. As for him, he would prefer it if she lowered her voice. Speaking Afrikaans in this country, he wants to tell her, is like speaking Nazi, if there were such a language.

He has made a mistake about their ages. They are not children at all: Ilse is twenty, Marianne twenty-one. They are in their final year at the University of the Orange Free State, both studying social work. He does not express an opinion, but to his mind social work – helping old women with their shopping – is not a subject a proper university would teach.

Marianne has never heard of computer programming and is incurious about it. But she does ask when he will be coming, as she puts it, home, *tuis*.

He does not know, he replies. Perhaps never. Is she not concerned about the direction in which South Africa is heading?

She gives a fling of the head. South Africa is not as bad as the English newspapers make out, she says. Blacks and whites would get along fine if they were just left alone. Anyway, she is not interested in politics.

He invites her to a film at the Everyman. It is Godard's *Bande à part*, which he has seen before but could see many times more, since it stars Anna Karina, with whom he is as much in love now as he was with Monica Vitti a year ago. Since it is not a highbrow film, or not obviously so, just a story about a gang of incompetent, amateurish criminals, he sees no reason why Marianne should not enjoy it.

Marianne is not a complainer, but throughout the film he can sense her fidgeting beside him. When he steals a glance, she is picking her fingernails, not watching the screen. Didn't you like it, he asks afterwards? I couldn't work out what it was about, she replies. It turns out she has never seen a film with subtitles.

He takes her back to his flat, or the flat that is his for the time being, for a cup of coffee. It is nearly eleven; Theodora has gone to bed. They sit cross-legged on the thick pile carpet in the living room, with the door shut, talking in low tones. She is not his cousin, but she is his cousin's friend, she is from home, and an air of illegitimacy hangs excitingly around her. He kisses her; she does not seem to mind being kissed. Face to face they stretch out on the carpet; he begins to unbutton, unlace, unzip her. The last train south is at 11.30. She will certainly miss it.

Marianne is a virgin. He finds this out when at last he has her naked in the big double bed. He has never slept with a virgin before, has never given a thought to virginity as a physical state. Now he learns his lesson. Marianne bleeds while they are making love and goes on bleeding afterwards. At the risk of waking the maid, she has to creep off to the bathroom to wash herself. While she is gone he switches on the light. There is blood on the sheets, blood all over his body. They have been – the vision comes to him distastefully – wallowing in blood like pigs.

She returns with a bathtowel wrapped around her. 'I must leave,' she says. 'The last train has gone,' he replies. 'Why don't you stay the night?'

The bleeding does not stop. Marianne falls asleep with the towel, growing more and more soggy, stuffed between her legs. He lies awake beside her fretting. Should he be calling an ambulance? Can he do so without waking Theodora? Marianne does not seem to be worried, but what if that is only pretence, for his sake? What if she is too innocent or too trustful to assess what is going on?

He is convinced he will not sleep, but he does. He is woken by voices and the sound of running water. It is five o'clock; already the birds are singing in the trees. Groggily he gets up and listens at the door: Theodora's voice, then Marianne's. What they are saying he cannot hear, but it cannot reflect well on him.

He strips off the bedclothes. The blood has soaked through to the mattress, leaving a huge, uneven stain. Guiltily, angrily, he heaves the mattress over. Only a matter of time before the stain is discovered. He must be gone by then, he will have to make sure of that.

Marianne returns from the bathroom wearing a robe that is not hers. She is taken aback by his silence, his cross looks. 'You never told me not to,' she says. 'Why shouldn't I talk to her? She's a nice old woman. A nice old *aia*.'

He telephones for a taxi, then waits pointedly at the front door while she dresses. When the taxi arrives he evades her embrace, puts a pound note in her hand. She regards it with puzzlement. 'I've got my own money,' she says. He shrugs, opens the door of the taxi for her.

For the remaining days of his tenancy he avoids Theodora. He leaves early in the morning, comes back late. If there are messages for him, he ignores them. When he took on the flat, he undertook to guard it from the husband and *be at hand*. He has failed in his undertaking once and is failing it again, but he does not care. The unsettling lovemaking, the whispering women, the bloody sheets, the stained mattress: he would like to put the whole shameful business behind him, close the book on it.

Muffling his voice, he calls the hostel in Earls Court and asks to speak to his cousin. She has left, they say, she and her friend. He puts the telephone down and relaxes. They are safely away, he need not face them again.

There remains the question of what to make of the episode, how to fit it into the story of his life that he tells himself. He has behaved dishonourably, no doubt about that, behaved like a cad. The word may be old-fashioned but it is exact. He deserves to be slapped in the face, even to be spat on. In the absence of anyone to administer the slap, he has no doubt that he will gnaw away at himself. *Agenbyte of inwit.* Let that be his contract then, with the gods: he will punish himself, and in return will hope the story of his caddish behaviour will not get out.

Yet what does it matter, finally, if the story does get out? He belongs to two worlds tightly sealed from each other. In the world of South Africa he is no more than a ghost, a wisp of smoke fast dwindling away, soon to have vanished for good. As for London, he is as good as unknown here. Already he has begun his search for new lodgings. When he has found a room he will break off contact with Theodora and the Merrington household and vanish into a sea of anonymity.

There is more to the sorry business, however, than just the shame of it. He has come to London to do what is impossible in South Africa: to explore the depths. Without descending into the depths one cannot be an artist. But what exactly are the depths? He had thought that trudging down icy streets, his heart numb with loneliness, was the depths. But perhaps the real depths are different, and come in unexpected form: in a flare-up of nastiness against a girl in the early hours of the morning, for instance. Perhaps the depths that he has wanted to plumb have been within him all the time, closed up in his chest: depths of coldness, callousness, caddishness. Does giving rein to his penchants, his vices, and then afterwards gnawing at himself, as he is doing now, help to qualify him to be an artist? He cannot, at this moment, see how.

At least the episode is closed, closed off, consigned to the past, sealed away in memory. But that is not true, not quite. A letter arrives postmarked Lucerne. Without second thought he opens it and begins to read. It is in Afrikaans. 'Dear John, I thought I should let you know that I am OK. Marianne is OK too. At first she did not understand why you did not phone, but after a while she cheered up, and we have been having a good time. She doesn't want to write, but I thought I would write anyway, to say I hope you don't treat all your girls like that, even in London. Marianne is a special person, she doesn't deserve that kind of treatment. You should think twice about the life you lead. Your cousin, Ilse.'

Even in London. What does she mean? That even by the standards of London he has behaved disgracefully? What do Ilse and her friend, fresh from the wastes of the Orange Free State, know about London and its standards? *London gets worse*, he wants to say. *If you would stay on for a while, instead of running away to the cowbells and the meadows, you might find that out for yourself.* But he does not really believe the fault is London's. He has read Henry James. He knows how easy it is to be bad, how one has only to relax for the badness to emerge.

The most hurtful moments in the letter are at the beginning and the end. *Beste John* is not how one addresses a family member, it is the way one addresses a stranger. And *Your cousin, Ilse*: who would have thought a farm girl capable of such a telling thrust!

For days and weeks, even after he has crumpled it up and thrown it away, his cousin's letter haunts him – not the actual words on the page, which he soon manages to blank out, but the memory of the moment when, despite having noticed the Swiss stamp and the childishly rounded handwriting, he slit open the envelope and read. What a fool! What was he expecting: a paean of thanks?

He does not like bad news. Particularly he does not like bad news about himself. *I am hard enough on myself*, he tells himself; *I do not need the help of others.* It is a sophistry he falls back on time and again to block his ears to criticism: he learned its usefulness when Jacqueline, from the perspective of a woman of thirty, gave him her opinion of him as a lover. Now, as soon as an affair begins to run out of steam, he withdraws. He abominates scenes, angry outbursts, home truths ('Do you want to know the truth about yourself?'), and does all in his power to evade them. What is truth anyway? If he is a mystery to himself, how can he be anything but a mystery to others? There is a pact he is ready to offer the women in his life: if they will treat him as a mystery, he will treat them as a closed book. On that basis and that alone will commerce be possible.

He is not a fool. As a lover his record is undistinguished, and he knows it. Never has he provoked in the heart of a woman what he would call a great passion. In fact, looking back, he cannot recall having been the object of a passion, a true passion, of any degree. That must say something about him. As for sex itself, narrowly understood, what he provides is, he suspects, rather meagre; and what he gets in return is meagre too. If the fault is anyone's, it is his own. For as long as he lacks heart, holds himself back, why should the woman not hold herself back too?

Is sex the measure of all things? If he fails in sex, does he fail the whole test of life? Things would be easier if that were not true. But when he looks around, he can see no one who does not stand in awe of the god of sex, except perhaps for a few dinosaurs, holdovers from Victorian times. Even Henry James, on the surface so proper, so Victorian, has pages where he darkly hints that everything, finally, is sex.

Of all the writers he follows, he trusts Pound the most. There is passion aplenty in Pound – the ache of longing, the fire of consummation – but it is passion untroubled, without a darker side. What is the key to Pound's equanimity? Is it that, as a worshipper of the Greek gods rather than the Hebrew god, he is immune to guilt? Or is Pound so steeped in great poetry that his physical being is in harmony with his emotions, a quality that communicates itself immediately to women and opens their hearts to him? Or, on the contrary, is Pound's secret simply a certain briskness in the conduct of life, a briskness to be attrib-uted to an American upbringing rather than to the gods or poetry, welcomed by women as a sign that the man knows what he wants and in a firm yet friendly way will take charge of where she and he are going? Is that what women want: to be taken charge of, to be led? Is that why dancers follow the code they do, the man leading, the woman following?

His own explanation for his failures in love, hoary by now and less and less to be trusted, is that he has yet to meet the right woman. The right woman will see through the opaque surface he presents to the world, to the depths inside; the right woman will unlock the hidden intensities of passion in him. Until that woman arrives, until that day of destiny, he is merely passing the time. That is why Marianne can be ignored.

One question still nags at him, and will not go away. Will the woman who unlocks the store of passion within him, if she exists, also release the blocked flow of poetry; or on the contrary is it up to him to turn himself into a poet and thus prove himself worthy of her love? It would be nice if the first were true, but he suspects it is not. Just as he has fallen in love at a distance with Ingeborg Bachmann in one way and with Anna Karina in another, so, he suspects, the intended one will have to know him by his works, to fall in love with his art before she will be so foolish as to fall in love with him.

SEVENTEEN

FROM PROFESSOR HOWARTH, his thesis supervisor back in Cape Town, he receives a letter requesting him to do some academic chores. Howarth is at work on a biography of the seventeenth-century playwright John Webster: he wants him to make copies of certain poems in the British Museum's manuscript collection that might have been written by Webster as a young man, and, while he is about it, of any manuscript poem he comes across signed 'I. W.' that sounds as if it might have been written by Webster.

Though the poems he finds himself reading are of no particular merit, he is flattered by the commission, with its implication that he will be able to recognize the author of *The Duchess of Malfi* by his style alone. From Eliot he has learned that the test of the critic is his ability to make fine discriminations. From Pound he has learned that the critic must be able to pick out the voice of the authentic master amid the babble of mere fashion. If he cannot play the piano, he can at least, when he switches on the radio, tell the difference between Bach and Telemann, Haydn and Mozart, Beethoven and Spohr, Bruckner and Mahler; if he cannot write, he at least possesses an ear that Eliot and Pound would approve of.

The question is, is Ford Madox Ford, on whom he is lavishing so much time, an authentic master? Pound promoted Ford as the sole heir in England of Henry James and Flaubert. But would Pound have been so sure of himself had he read the whole Ford oeuvre? If Ford was such a fine writer, why, mixed in with his five good novels, is there so much rubbish?

Though he is supposed to be writing about Ford's fiction, he finds Ford's minor novels less interesting than his books about France. To Ford there can be no greater happiness than to pass one's days by the side of a good woman in a sunlit house in the south of France, with an olive tree at the back door and a good *vin de pays* in the cellar. Provence, says Ford, is the cradle of all that is gracious and lyrical and humane in European civilization; as for the women of Provence, with their fiery temperament and their aquiline good looks they put the women of the north to shame.

Is Ford to be believed? Will he himself ever see Provence? Will the fiery Provençal women pay any attention to him, with his notable lack of fire?

Ford says that the civilization of Provence owes its lightness and grace to a diet of fish and olive oil and garlic. In his new lodgings in Highgate, out of deference to Ford, he buys fish fingers instead of sausages, fries them in olive oil instead of butter, sprinkles garlic salt over them.

The thesis he is writing will have nothing new to say about Ford, that has become clear. Yet he does not want to abandon it. Giving up undertakings is his father's way. He is not going to be like his father. So he commences the task of reducing his hundreds of pages of notes in tiny handwriting to a web of connected prose.

On days when, sitting in the great, domed Reading Room, he finds himself too exhausted or bored to write any more, he allows himself the luxury of dipping into books about the South

Africa of the old days, books to be found only in great libraries, memoirs of visitors to the Cape like Dapper and Kolbe and Sparrman and Barrow and Burchell, published in Holland or Germany or England two centuries ago.

It gives him an eerie feeling to sit in London reading about streets — Waalstraat, Buitengracht, Buitencingel — along which he alone, of all the people around him with their heads buried in their books, has walked. But even more than by accounts of old Cape Town is he captivated by stories of ventures into the interior, reconnaissances by ox-wagon into the desert of the Great Karoo, where a traveller could trek for days on end without clapping eyes on a living soul. Zwartberg, Leeuwrivier, Dwyka: it is his country, the country of his heart, that he is reading about.

Patriotism: is that what is beginning to afflict him? Is he proving himself unable to live without a country? Having shaken the dust of the ugly new South Africa from his feet, is he yearning for the South Africa of the old days, when Eden was still possible? Do these Englishmen around him feel the same tug at the heartstrings when there is mention of Rydal Mount or Baker Street in a book? He doubts it. This country, this city, are by now wrapped in centuries of words. Englishmen do not find it at all strange to be walking in the footsteps of Chaucer or Tom Jones.

South Africa is different. Were it not for this handful of books, he could not be sure he had not dreamed up the Karoo yesterday. That is why he pores over Burchell in particular, in his two heavy volumes. Burchell may not be a master like Flaubert or James, but what Burchell writes really happened. Real oxen hauled him and his cases of botanical specimens from stopping-place to stopping-place in the Great Karoo; real stars glimmered above his head, and his men's, while they slept. It dizzies him even to think about it. Burchell and his men may be dead, and their wagons turned to dust, but they really lived, their travels were real travels. The proof is the book he holds in his hands, the book called for short *Burchell's Travels*, in specific the copy lodged in the British Museum.

If Burchell's travels are proved real by *Burchell's Travels*, why should other books not make other travels real, travels that are as yet only hypothetical? The logic is of course false. Nevertheless, he would like to do it: write a book as convincing as Burchell's and lodge it in this library that defines all libraries. If, to make his book convincing, there needs to be a grease-pot swinging under the bed of the wagon as it bumps across the stones of the Karoo, he will do the grease-pot. If there have to be cicadas trilling in the tree under which they stop at noon, he will do the cicadas. The creak of the grease-pot, the trilling of the cicadas – those he is confident he can bring off. The difficult part will be to give to the whole the aura that will get it onto the shelves and thus into the history of the world: the aura of truth.

It is not forgery he is contemplating. People have tried that route before: pretended to find, in a chest in an attic in a country-house, a journal, yellow with age, stained with damp, describing an expedition across the deserts of Tartary or into the territories of the Great Moghul. Deceptions of that kind do not interest him. The challenge he faces is a purely literary one: to write a book whose horizon of knowledge will be that of Burchell's time, the 1820s, yet whose response to the world around it will be alive in a way that Burchell, despite his energy and intelligence and curiosity and sang-froid, could not be because he was an Englishman in a foreign country, his mind half occupied with Pembrokeshire and the sisters he had left behind.

He will have to school himself to write from within the

1820s. Before he can bring that off he will need to know less than he knows now; he will need to forget things. Yet before he can forget he will have to know what to forget; before he can know less he will have to know more. Where will he find what he needs to know? He has no training as an historian, and anyway what he is after will not be in history books, since it belongs to the mundane, a mundane as common as the air one breathes. Where will he find the common knowledge of a bygone world, a knowledge too humble to know it is knowledge?

EIGHTEEN

WHAT HAPPENS NEXT happens swiftly. In the mail on the table in the hallway there appears a buff envelope marked OHMS, addressed to him. He takes it to his room and with a sinking heart opens it. He has twenty-one days, the letter tells him, in which to renew his work permit, failing which permission to reside in the United Kingdom will be withdrawn. He may renew the permit by presenting himself, his passport, and a copy of Form I-48, completed by his employer, at the Home Office premises on Holloway Road on any weekday between the hours of 9.00 and 12.30, and 1.30 and 4.00.

So IBM has betrayed him. IBM has told the Home Office he has left their employ.

What must he do? He has enough money for a one-way ticket back to South Africa. But it is inconceivable that he should reappear in Cape Town like a dog with its tail between its legs, defeated. What is there for him to do in Cape Town anyway? Resume his tutoring at the University? How long can that go on? He is too old by now for scholarships, he would be competing against younger students with better records. The fact is, if he goes back to South Africa he will never escape again. He will become like the people who gather on Clifton beach in the evenings to drink wine and tell each other about the old days on Ibiza.

If he wants to stay on in England, there are two avenues he can see open to him. He can grit his teeth and try schoolmastering again; or he can go back to computer programming.

There is a third option, hypothetical. He can quit his present address and melt into the masses. He can go hop-picking in Kent (one does not need papers for that), work on building sites. He can sleep in youth hostels, in barns. But he knows he will do none of this. He is too incompetent to lead a life outside the law, too prim, too afraid of getting caught.

The job listings in the newspapers are full of appeals for computer programmers. England cannot, it would seem, find enough of them. Most are for openings in payroll departments. These he ignores, responding only to the computer companies themselves, the rivals, great and small, of IBM. Within days he has had an interview with International Computers, and, without hesitation, accepted their offer. He is exultant. He is employed again, he is safe, he is not going to be ordered out of the country.

There is one catch. Though International Computers has its head office in London, the work for which they want him is out in the country, in Berkshire. It takes a trip to Waterloo, followed by a one-hour train journey, followed by a bus ride, to get there. It will not be possible to live in London. It is the Rothamsted story all over again.

International Computers is prepared to lend new employees the down payment on an appropriately modest home. In other words, with a stroke of a pen he can become a houseowner (he! a houseowner!) and by the same act commit himself to mortgage repayments that would bind him to his job for the next ten or fifteen years. In fifteen years he will be an old man. A single rushed decision and he will have signed away his life, signed away all chance of becoming an artist. With a little house of his own in a row of redbrick houses, he will be absorbed without trace into the British middle class. All that will be needed to complete the picture will be a little wife and car.

He finds an excuse not to sign up for the house loan. Instead he signs a lease on a flat on the top floor of a house on the fringes of the town. The landlord is an ex-Army officer, now a stockbroker, who likes to be addressed as Major Arkwright. To Major Arkwright he explains what computers are, what computer programming is, what a solid career it affords ('There is bound to be huge expansion in the industry'). Major Arkwright jocularly calls him a boffin ('We've never had a boffin in the upstairs flat before'), a designation he accepts without murmur.

Working for International Computers is quite unlike working for IBM. To begin with, he can pack his black suit away. He has an office of his own, a cubicle in a Quonset hut in the back garden of the house that International Computers has outfitted as its computing laboratory. 'The Manor House': that is what they call it, a rambling old building at the end of a leaf-strewn driveway two miles outside Bracknell. Presumably it has a history, though no one knows what that history is.

Despite the designation 'Computing Laboratory,' there is no actual computer on the premises. To test the programs he is being hired to write, he will have to travel to Cambridge University, which owns one of the three Atlas computers, the only three in existence, each slightly different from the others. The Atlas computer – so he reads in the brief placed before him on his first morning – is Britain's reply to IBM. Once the engineers and programmers of International Computers have got these prototypes running, Atlas will be the biggest computer in the world, or at least the biggest that can be bought on the open market (the American military have computers of their own, of unrevealed power, and presumably the Russian military too). Atlas will strike a blow for the British computer industry from which IBM will take years to recover. That is what is at stake. That is why International Computers has assembled a team of bright young programmers, of whom he has now become one, in this rural retreat.

What is special about Atlas, what makes it unique among the world's computers, is that it has self-consciousness of a kind. At regular intervals – every ten seconds, or even every second – it interrogates itself, asking itself what tasks it is performing and whether it is performing them with optimal efficiency. If it is not performing efficiently, it will rearrange its tasks and carry them out in a different, better order, thus saving time, which is money.

It will be his task to write the routine for the machine to follow at the end of each swing of the magnetic tape. Should it read another swing of tape, it must ask itself? Or should it, on the contrary, break off and read a punched card or a strip of paper tape? Should it write some of the output that has accumulated onto another magnetic tape, or should it do a burst of computing? These questions are to be answered according to the overriding principle of efficiency. He will have as much time as he needs (but preferably only six months, since International Computers is in a race against time) to reduce questions and answers to machine-readable code and test that they are optimally formulated. Each of his fellow programmers has a comparable task and a similar schedule. Meanwhile, engineers at the University of Manchester will be working day and night to perfect the electronic hardware. If all goes according to plan, Atlas will go into production in 1965.

A race against time. A race against the Americans. That is something he can understand, something he can commit himself to more wholeheartedly than he could commit himself to IBM's goal of making more and more money. And the programming itself is interesting. It requires mental ingenuity; it requires, if it is to be well done, a virtuoso command of Atlas's two-level internal language. He arrives for work in the mornings looking forward to the tasks that await him. To stay alert he drinks cup after cup of coffee; his heart hammers, his brain seethes; he loses track of time, has to be called to lunch. In the evenings he takes his papers back to his rooms at Major Arkwright's and works into the night.

So this is what, unbeknown to myself, I was preparing for, he thinks! So this is where mathematics leads one!

Autumn turns to winter; he is barely aware of it. He is no longer reading poetry. Instead he reads books on chess, follows grandmaster games, does the chess problems in the *Observer*. He sleeps badly; sometimes he dreams about programming. It is a development within himself that he watches with detached interest. Will he become like those scientists whose brains solve problems while they sleep?

There is another thing he notices. He has stopped yearning. The quest for the mysterious, beautiful stranger who will set free the passion within him no longer preoccupies him. In part, no doubt, that is because Bracknell offers nothing to match the parade of girls in London. But he cannot help seeing a connection between the end of yearning and the end of poetry. Does it mean he is growing up? Is that what growing up amounts to: growing out of yearning, of passion, of all intensities of the soul?

The people among whom he works – men, without exception – are more interesting than the people at IBM: more lively, and perhaps cleverer too, in a way he can understand, a way that is much like being clever at school. They have lunch together in the canteen of the Manor House. There is no nonsense about the food they are served: fish and chips, bangers and mash, toad in the hole, bubble and squeak, rhubarb tart with ice cream. He likes the food, has two helpings if he can, makes it the main meal of the day. In the evenings, at home (if that is what they are now, his rooms at the Arkwrights'), he does not bother to cook, simply eats bread and cheese over the chessboard.

Among his co-workers is an Indian named Ganapathy. Ganapathy often arrives late to work; on some days he does not come at all. When he does come, he does not appear to be working very hard: he sits in his cubicle with his feet on the desk, apparently dreaming. For his absences he has only the most cursory of excuses ('I was not well'). Nevertheless, he is not chided. Ganapathy, it emerges, is a particularly valuable acquisition for International Computers. He has studied in America, holds an American degree in computer science.

He and Ganapathy are the two foreigners in the group. Together, when the weather allows, they go for after-lunch strolls in the manor grounds. Ganapathy is disparaging about International Computers and the whole Atlas project. Coming back to England was a mistake on his part, he says. The English do not know how to think big. He should have stayed in America. What is life like in South Africa? Would there be prospects for him in South Africa?

He dissuades Ganapathy from trying South Africa. South Africa is very backward, he tells him, there are no computers there. He does not tell him that outsiders are not welcome unless they are white.

A bad spell sets in, day after day of rain and blustery wind. Ganapathy does not come to work at all. Since no one else asks why, he takes it upon himself to investigate. Like him, Ganapathy has evaded the home-ownership option. He lives in a flat on the third floor of a council block. For a long while there is no answer to his knocking. Then Ganapathy opens the door. He is wearing pyjamas and sandals; from the interior comes a gush of steamy warmth and a smell of rottenness. 'Come in, come in!' says Ganapathy. 'Come out of the cold!'

There is no furniture in the living room except for a television set with an armchair before it, and two blazing electric heaters. Behind the door is a pile of black rubbish bags. It is from them that the bad smell comes. With the door closed the smell is quite nauseating. 'Why don't you take the bags out?' he asks. Ganapathy is evasive. Nor will he say why he has not been to work. In fact, he does not appear to want to talk at all.

He wonders whether Ganapathy has a girl in the bedroom, a local girl, one of the pert little typists or shop assistants from the housing estate whom he sees on the bus. Or perhaps, indeed, an Indian girl. Perhaps that is the explanation for all of Ganapathy's absences: there is a beautiful Indian girl living with him, and he prefers making love to her, practising Tantra, deferring orgasm for hours on end, to writing machine code for Atlas.

When he makes a move to leave, however, Ganapathy shakes his head. 'Would you like some water?' he offers.

Ganapathy offers him tap-water because he has run out of tea and coffee. He has also run out of food. He does not buy food, except for bananas, because, it emerges, he does not cook – does not like cooking, does not know how to cook. The rubbish bags contain, for the most part, banana peels. That is what he lives on: bananas, chocolates, and, when he has it, tea. It is not the way he would like to live. In India he lived at home, and his mother and sisters took care of him. In America, in Columbus, Ohio, he lived in what he calls a dormitory, where food appeared on the table at regular intervals. If you were hungry between meals you went out and bought a hamburger. There was a hamburger place open twenty-four hours a day on

146

the street outside the dormitory. In America things were always open, not like in England. He should never have come back to England, a country without a future where even the heating does not work.

He asks Ganapathy whether he is ill. Ganapathy brushes aside his concern: he wears the dressing-gown for warmth, that is all. But he is not convinced. Now that he knows about the bananas, he sees Ganapathy with new eyes. Ganapathy is as tiny as a sparrow, with not a spare ounce of flesh. His face is gaunt. If he is not ill, he is at least starving. Behold: in Bracknell, in the heart of the Home Counties, a man is starving because he is too incompetent to feed himself.

He invites Ganapathy to lunch the next day, giving him precise instructions for how to get to Major Arkwright's. Then he goes out, searches for a shop that is open on a Saturday afternoon, and buys what it has to offer: bread in a plastic wrapper, cold meats, frozen green peas. At noon the next day he lays out the repast and waits. Ganapathy does not arrive. Since Ganapathy does not have a telephone, there is nothing he can do about it short of conveying the meal to Ganapathy's flat.

Absurd, but perhaps that is what Ganapathy wants: to have his food brought to him. Like himself, Ganapathy is a spoiled, clever boy. Like himself, Ganapathy has run away from his mother and the smothering ease she offers. But in Ganapathy's case, running away seems to have used up all his energy. Now he is waiting to be rescued. He wants his mother, or someone like her, to come and save him. Otherwise he will simply waste away and die, in his flat full of garbage.

International Computers ought to hear about this. Ganapathy has been entrusted with a key task, the logic of the job-scheduling routines. If Ganapathy falls out, the whole Atlas project will be delayed. But how can International Computers be made to understand what ails Ganapathy? How can anyone in England understand what brings people from the far corners of the earth to die on a wet, miserable island which they detest and to which they have no ties?

The next day Ganapathy is at his desk as usual. For the missed appointment he offers no word of explanation. At lunchtime, in the canteen, he is in good spirits, even excited. He has entered a raffle for a Morris Mini, he says. He has bought a hundred tickets – what else should he do with the big salary International Computers pays him? If he wins, they can drive to Cambridge together to do their program testing, instead of catching trains. Or they can drive to London for the day.

Is there something about the whole business that he has failed to understand, something Indian? Does Ganapathy belong to a caste to which it is taboo to eat at the table of a Westerner? If so, what is he doing with a plate of cod and chips in the Manor House canteen? Should the invitation to lunch have been made more formally and confirmed in writing? By not arriving, was Ganapathy graciously saving him the embarrassment of finding a guest at his front door whom he had invited on an impulse but did not really want? Did he somehow give the impression, when he invited Ganapathy, that it was not a real, substantial invitation he was extending, merely a gesture toward an invitation, and that true politeness on Ganapathy's part would consist in acknowledging the gesture without putting his host to the trouble of providing a repast? Does the notional meal (cold meats and boiled frozen peas with butter) that they would have eaten together have the same value, in the transaction between himself and Ganapathy, as cold meats and boiled frozen peas actually offered and consumed? Is everything between himself and Ganapathy as before, or better than before, or worse?

Ganapathy has heard about Satyajit Ray but does not think

he has seen any of his films. Only a tiny sector of the Indian public, he says, would be interested in such films. In general, he says, Indians prefer to watch American films. Indian films are still very primitive.

Ganapathy is the first Indian he has known more than casually, if this can be called knowing – chess games and conversations comparing England unfavourably with America, plus the one surprise visit to Ganapathy's flat. Conversation would no doubt improve if Ganapathy were an intellectual instead of being just clever. It continues to astound him that people can be as clever as people are in the computer industry, yet have no outside interests beyond cars and house prices. He had thought it was just the notorious philistinism of the English middle class manifesting itself, but Ganapathy is no better.

Is this indifference to the world a consequence of too much intercourse with machines that give the appearance of thinking? How would he fare if one day he were to quit the computer industry and rejoin civilized society? After spending his best energies for so long on games with machines, would he be able to hold his own in conversation? Is there anything he would have gained from years with computers? Would he not at least have learned to think logically? Would logic not by then have become his second nature?

He would like to believe so, but he cannot. Finally he has no respect for any version of thinking that can be embodied in a computer's circuitry. The more he has to do with computing, the more it seems to him like chess: a tight little world defined by made-up rules, one that sucks in boys of a certain susceptible temperament and turns them half-crazy, as he is half-crazy, so that all the time they deludedly think they are playing the game, the game is in fact playing them.

It is a world he can escape – it is not too late for that.

Alternatively he can make his peace with it, as he sees the young men around him do, one by one: settle for marriage and a house and car, settle for what life realistically has to offer, sink their energies in their work. He is chagrined to see how well the reality principle operates, how, under the prod of loneliness, the boy with spots settles for the girl with the dull hair and the heavy legs, how everyone, no matter how unlikely, finds, in the end, a partner, Is that his problem, and is it as simple as that: that all the time he has been overestimating his worth on the market, fooling himself into believing he belongs with sculptresses and actresses when he really belongs with the kindergarten teacher on the housing estate or the apprentice manageress of the shoe store?

Marriage: who would have imagined he would be feeling the tug, however faint, of marriage! He is not going to give in, not yet. But it is an option he plays with on the long winter evenings, eating his bread and sausages in front of Major Arkwright's gas fire, listening to the radio, while the rain patters in the background against the window.

NINETEEN

IT IS RAINING. He and Ganapathy are alone in the canteen, playing lightning chess on Ganapathy's pocket set. Ganapathy is beating him, as usual.

'You should go to America,' says Ganapathy. 'You are wasting your time here. We are all wasting our time.'

He shakes his head. 'That's not realistic,' he replies.

He has thought more than once of trying for a job in America, and decided against it. A prudent decision, but a correct one. As a programmer he has no particular gifts. His colleagues on the Atlas team may not have advanced degrees, but their minds are clearer than his, their grasp of computational problems is quicker and keener than his will ever be. In discussion he can barely hold his own; he is always having to pretend to understand when he does not really understand, and then work things out for himself afterwards. Why should businesses in America want someone like him? America is not England. America is hard and merciless: if by some miracle he bluffed his way into a job there, he would soon be found out. Besides, he has read Allen Ginsberg, read William Burroughs. He knows what America does to artists: sends them mad, locks them up, drives them out.

'You could get a fellowship at a university,' says Ganapathy. 'I got one, you would have no trouble.'

He stares hard. Is Ganapathy really such an innocent? There is a Cold War on the go. America and Russia are competing for the hearts and minds of Indians, Iraquis, Nigerians; scholarships to universities are among the inducements they offer. The hearts and minds of whites are of no interest to them, certainly not the hearts and minds of a few out-of-place whites in Africa.

'I'll think about it,' he says, and changes the subject. He has no intention of thinking about it.

In a photograph on the front page of the *Guardian* a Vietnamese soldier in American-style uniform stares helplessly into a sea of flames. 'SUICIDE BOMBERS WREAK HAVOC IN S. VIETNAM,' reads the headline. A band of Viet-Cong sappers have cut their way through the barbed wire around the American air base at Pleiku, blown up twenty-four aircraft, and set fire to the fuel storage tanks. They have given up their lives in the action.

Ganapathy, who shows him the newspaper, is exultant; he himself feels a surge of vindication. Ever since he arrived in England the British newspapers and BBC have carried stories of American feats of arms in which Viet-Cong are killed by the thousand while the Americans get away unscathed. If there is ever a word of criticism of America, it is of the most muted kind. He can barely bring himself to read the war reports, so much do they sicken him. Now the Viet-Cong have given their undeniable, heroic reply.

He and Ganapathy have never discussed Vietnam. Because Ganapathy studied in America, he has assumed that Ganapathy either supports the Americans or is as indifferent to the war as everyone else at International Computers. Now, suddenly, in his smile, the glint in his eye, he is seeing Ganapathy's secret face. Despite his admiration for American efficiency and his longing for American hamburgers, Ganapathy is on the side of the Vietnamese because they are his Asian brothers.

That is all. That is the end of it. There is no further mention of the war between them. But he wonders more than ever what Ganapathy is doing in England, in the Home Counties, working on a project he has no respect for. Would he not be better off in Asia, fighting the Americans? Should he have a chat to him, tell him so?

And what of himself? If Ganapathy's destiny lies in Asia, where does his lie? Would the Viet-Cong ignore his origins and accept his services, if not as a soldier or suicide bomber then as a humble porter? If not, what of the friends and allies of the Viet-Cong, the Chinese?

He writes to the Chinese Embassy in London. Since he suspects the Chinese have no use for computers, he says nothing about computer programming. He is prepared to come and teach English in China, he says, as a contribution to the world struggle. What he is paid is of no importance to him.

He mails the letter and waits for a reply. Meanwhile he buys *Teach Yourself Chinese* and begins to practise the strange clenched-teeth sounds of Mandarin.

Day after day passes; from the Chinese there is no word. Have the British secret services intercepted his letter and destroyed it? Do they intercept and destroy all letters to the Embassy? If so, what is the point in letting the Chinese have an embassy in London? Or, having intercepted his letter, have the secret services forwarded it to the Home Office with a note to say that the South African working for International Computers in Bracknell has betrayed communist leanings? Is he going to lose his job and be expelled from England on account of politics? If it happens, he will not contest it. Fate will have spoken; he is prepared to accept the word of fate.

On his trips to London he still goes to the cinema, but his

pleasure is more and more spoiled by the deterioration of his eyesight. He has to sit in the front row to be able to read the subtitles, and even then he must screw up his eyes and strain.

He visits an ophthalmologist and comes away with a pair of black horn-rimmed spectacles. In the mirror he resembles even more closely Major Arkwright's comic boffin. On the other hand, looking out through the window he is amazed to discover he can make out individual leaves on the trees. Trees have been a blur of green ever since he can remember. Should he have been wearing glasses all his life? Does this explain why he was so bad at cricket, why the ball always seemed to be coming at him out of nowhere?

We end up looking like our ideal selves, says Baudelaire. The face we are born with is slowly overwhelmed by the desired face, the face of our secret dreams. Is the face in the mirror the face of his dreams, this long, lugubrious face with the soft, vulnerable mouth and now the blank eyes shielded behind glass?

The first film he sees with his new glasses is Pasolini's *Gospel According to St Matthew*. It is an unsettling experience. After five years of Catholic schooling he had thought he was forever beyond the appeal of the Christian message. But he is not. The pale, bony Jesus of the film, shrinking back from the touch of others, striding about barefoot issuing prophecies and fulminations, is real in a way that Jesus of the bleeding heart never was. He winces when nails are hammered through the hands of Jesus; when his tomb is revealed to be empty and the angel announces to the mourning women, 'Look not here, for he is risen,' and the Missa Luba bursts out and the common folk of the land, the halt and the maimed, the despised and rejected, come running or hobbling, their faces alight with joy, to share in the good news, his own heart wants to burst; tears of an exultation he does not understand stream down his cheeks, tears that he has surreptitiously to wipe away before he can emerge into the world again.

In the window of a second-hand bookseller off Charing Cross Road, on another of his expeditions to the city, he spots a chunky little book with a violet cover: *Watt*, by Samuel Beckett, published by Olympia Press. Olympia Press is notorious: from a safe haven in Paris it publishes pornography in English for subscribers in England and America. But as a sideline it also publishes the more daring writings of the avant-garde – Vladimir Nabokov's *Lolita*, for instance. It is hardly likely that Samuel Beckett, author of *Waiting for Godot* and *Endgame*, writes pornography. What kind of book, then, is *Watt*?

He pages through it. It is printed in the same fullbodied serif type as Pound's *Selected Poems*, a type that evokes for him intimacy, solidity. He buys the book and takes it back to Major Arkwright's. From the first page he knows he has hit on something. Propped up in bed with light pouring through the window, he reads and reads.

Watt is quite unlike Beckett's plays. There is no clash, no conflict, just the flow of a voice telling a story, a flow continually checked by doubts and scruples, its pace fitted exactly to the pace of his own mind. *Watt* is also funny, so funny that he rolls about laughing. When he comes to the end he starts again at the beginning.

Why did people not tell him Beckett wrote novels? How could he have imagined he wanted to write in the manner of Ford when Beckett was around all the time? In Ford there has always been an element of the stuffed shirt that he has disliked but has been hesitant to acknowledge, something to do with the value Ford placed on knowing where in the West End to buy the best motoring gloves or how to tell a Médoc from a Beaune; whereas Beckett is classless, or outside class, as he himself would prefer to be.

★   ★   ★

The testing of the programs they write has to be done on the Atlas machine in Cambridge, during the night hours when the mathematicians who enjoy first claim on it are sleeping. So every second or third week he catches the train to Cambridge, carrying a satchel with his papers and his rolls of punched tape and his pyjamas and his toothbrush. While in Cambridge he resides at the Royal Hotel, at International Computers' expense. From six in the evening until six in the morning he works on Atlas. In the early morning he returns to the hotel, has breakfast, and retires to bed. In the afternoon he is free to wander around the town, perhaps going to a film. Then it is time to return to the Mathematical Laboratory, the huge, hangar-like building that houses Atlas, for the night's stint.

It is a routine that suits him down to the ground. He likes train trips, likes the anonymity of hotel rooms, likes huge English breakfasts of bacon and sausages and eggs and toast and marmalade and coffee. Since he does not have to wear a suit, he can mix easily with students on the street, even seem to be one of them. And being with the huge Atlas machine all night, alone save for the duty engineer, watching the roll of computer code that *he* has written speed through the tape reader, watching the magnetic tape disks begin to spin and the lights on the console begin to flash at *his* command, gives him a sense of power that he knows is childish but that, with no one watching, he can safely revel in.

Sometimes he has to stay on at the Mathematical Laboratory into the morning to confer with members of the mathematics department. For everything that is truly novel about the Atlas software comes not from International Computers but from a handful of mathematicians at Cambridge. From a certain point of view, he is merely one of a team of professional programmers from the computer industry that the Cambridge Mathematics

Department has hired to implement its ideas, just as from the same point of view International Computers is a firm of engineers hired by Manchester University to build a computer according to its design. From that point of view, he himself is merely a skilled workman in the pay of the university, not a collaborator entitled to speak on an equal footing with these brilliant young scientists.

For brilliant they are indeed. Sometimes he shakes his head in disbelief at what is happening. Here he is, an undistinguished graduate from a second-class university in the colonies, being permitted to address by first name men with doctorates in mathematics, men who, once they get talking, leave him dizzied in their wake. Problems over which he has dully wrestled for weeks are solved by them in a flash. More often than not, behind what he had thought were problems they see what are the *real* problems, which they pretend for his sake he has seen too.

Are these men truly so lost in the higher reaches of computational logic that they do not see how stupid he is; or — for reasons that are dark to him, since he must count as nothing to them — are they graciously seeing to it that he does not lose face in their company? Is that what civilization is: an unwhispered agreement that no one, no matter how insignificant, should be allowed to lose face? He can believe it of Japan; does it hold for England too? Whatever the case, how truly admirable!

He is in Cambridge, on the premises of an ancient university, hobnobbing with the great. He has even been given a key to the Mathematical Laboratory, a key to the side door, to let himself in and out. What more could he hope for? But he must be wary of getting carried away, of getting inflated ideas. He is here by luck and nothing else. He could never have studied at Cambridge, was never good enough to win a scholarship. He must continue to think of himself as a hired hand: if not, he will become an impostor in the same way that Jude Fawley amid the dreaming spires of Oxford was an impostor. One of these days, quite soon, his tasks will be done, he will have to give back his key, the visits to Cambridge will cease. But let him at least enjoy them while he can.

TWENTY

HE IS INTO his third summer in England. After lunch, on the lawn behind the Manor House, he and the other programmers have taken to playing cricket with a tennis ball and an old bat found in a broom closet. He has not played cricket since he left school, when he decided to renounce it on the grounds that team sports were incompatible with the life of a poet and an intellectual. Now he finds to his surprise how much he still enjoys the game. Not only does he enjoy it, he is good at it. All the strokes he strove as a child so ineffectually to master come back unbidden, with an ease and fluency that are new because his arms are stronger and because there is no reason to be frightened of the soft ball. He is better, much better, as a batsman and as a bowler too, than his fellow players. How, he asks himself, did these young Englishmen spend their school days? Must he, a colonial, teach them to play their own game?

His obsession with chess is waning, he is beginning to read again. Though the Bracknell library in itself is tiny and inadequate, the librarians are ready to order him any book he wants from the county network. He is reading in the history of logic, pursuing an intuition that logic is a human invention, not part of the fabric of being, and therefore (there are many intermediate steps, but he can fill them in later) that computers are simply toys invented by boys (led by Charles Babbage) for the amusement of other boys. There are many alternative logics, he is convinced (but how many?), each just as good as the logic of *either-or*. The threat of the toy by which he earns his living, the threat that makes it more than just a toy, is that it will burn *either-or* paths in the brains of its users and thus lock them irreversibly into its binary logic.

He pores over Aristotle, over Peter Ramus, over Rudolf Carnap. Most of what he reads he does not understand, but he is used to not understanding. All he is searching for at present is the moment in history when *either-or* is chosen and *and/or* discarded.

He has his books and his projects (the Ford thesis, now nearing completion, the dismantling of logic) for the empty evenings, cricket at midday, and, every second week, a spell at the Royal Hotel with the luxury of nights alone with Atlas, the most redoubtable computer in the world. Could a bachelor's life, if it has to be a bachelor's life, be any better?

There is only one shadow. A year has passed since he last wrote a line of poetry. What has happened to him? Is it true that art comes only out of misery? Must he become miserable again in order to write? Does there not also exist a poetry of ecstasy, even a poetry of lunchtime cricket as a form of ecstasy? Does it matter where poetry finds its impetus as long as it is poetry?

Although Atlas is not a machine built to handle textual materials, he uses the dead hours of the night to get it to print out thousands of lines in the style of Pablo Neruda, using as a lexicon a list of the most powerful words in *The Heights of Macchu Picchu*, in Nathaniel Tarn's translation. He brings the thick wad of paper back to the Royal Hotel and pores over it. 'The nostalgia of teapots.' 'The ardour of shutters.' 'Furious horsemen.' If he cannot, for the present, write poetry that comes from the heart, if his heart is not in the right state to generate poetry of its own, can he at least string together pseudo-poems made up of phrases generated by a machine, and thus, by going through the motions of writing, learn again to write? Is it fair to be using mechanical aids to writing – fair to other poets, fair to the dead masters? The Surrealists wrote words on slips of paper and shook them up in a hat and drew words at random to make up lines. William Burroughs cuts up pages and shuffles them and puts the bits together. Is he not doing the same kind of thing? Or do his huge resources – what other poet in England, in the world, has a machine of this size at his command – turn quantity into quality? Yet might it not be argued that the invention of computers has changed the nature of art, by making the author and the condition of the author's heart irrelevant? On the Third Programme he has heard music from the studios of Radio Cologne, music spliced together from electronic whoops and crackles and street noise and snippets of old recordings and fragments of speech. Is it not time for poetry to catch up with music?

He sends a selection of his Neruda poems to a friend in Cape Town, who publishes them in a magazine he edits. A local newspaper reprints one of the computer poems with a derisive commentary. For a day or two, back in Cape Town, he is notorious as the barbarian who wants to replace Shakespeare with a machine.

Besides the Atlas computers in Cambridge and Manchester, there is a third Atlas. It is housed at the Ministry of Defence's atomic weapons research station outside Aldermaston, not far from Bracknell. Once the software that runs Atlas has been tested in Cambridge and found good, it has to be installed on the

Aldermaston machine. Assigned to instal it are the programmers who wrote it. But first these programmers have to pass a security check. Each is given a long questionnaire to fill in about his family, his personal history, his work experience; each is visited at home by men who introduce themselves as from the police but are more likely from Military Intelligence.

All the British programmers are cleared and given cards to wear around their necks during visits, with their photographs on them. Once they have presented themselves at the entrance to Aldermaston and been escorted to the computer building, they are left more or less free to move around as they please.

For Ganapathy and himself, however, there is no question of clearance, since they are foreigners, or, as Ganapathy qualifies it, non-American foreigners. At the entrance gate the two of them therefore have guards assigned to them individually, who conduct them from place to place, stand watch over them at all times, and refuse to be engaged in conversation. When they go to the toilet, their guard stands at the cubicle door; when they eat, their guard stands behind them. They are allowed to speak to other International Computers personnel but to no one else.

His involvement with Mr Pomfret in the IBM days, and his part in furthering the development of the TSR-2 bomber, seem in retrospect so trivial, even comic, that his conscience is easily set at rest. Aldermaston is a different kettle of fish. He spends a total of ten days there, over a period of weeks. By the time he is finished, the tape-scheduling routines are working as well as they work at Cambridge. His task is done. Doubtless there are other people who could have installed the routines, but not as well as he, who wrote them and knows them inside out. Other people could have done the job, but other people did not. Though he could have made a case for being excused (he could, for instance, have pointed to the unnatural circumstance of being observed in all his actions by a poker-faced guard, and the effect of that on his state of mind), he did not make such a case. Mr Pomfret may have been a joke, but he cannot pretend Aldermaston is a joke.

He has never known a place like Aldermaston. In atmosphere it is quite unlike Cambridge. The cubicle where he works, as with every other cubicle and everything inside them, is cheap, functional, and ugly. The whole base, made up of low, scattered brick buildings, is ugly with the ugliness of a place that knows no one will look at it or care to look at it; perhaps with the ugliness of a place that knows, when war comes, it will be blown off the face of the earth.

No doubt there are clever people here, as clever as the Cambridge mathematicians, or nearly so. No doubt some of the people he glimpses in the corridors, Operations Supervisors, Research Officers, Technical Officers Grades I, II and III, Senior Technical Officers, people he is not allowed to speak to, are themselves graduates of Cambridge. He has written the routines he is installing, but the planning behind them was done by Cambridge people, people who could not have been unaware that the machine in the Mathematical Laboratory had a sinister sister at Aldermaston. The hands of the people at Cambridge are not a great deal cleaner than his own hands. Nevertheless, by passing through these gates, by breathing the air here, he has aided the arms race, become an accomplice in the Cold War, and on the wrong side too.

Tests no longer seem to come with fair warning these days, as they did when he was a schoolboy, or even to announce themselves as tests. But in this case it is hard to plead unpreparedness as an excuse. From the moment the word *Aldermaston* was first uttered he knew Aldermaston would be a test and knew he was not going to pass, was going to lack what it took to pass. By working at Aldermaston he has lent himself to evil, and, from a certain point of view, lent himself more culpably than his English colleagues, who if they had refused to participate would have risked their careers far more seriously than he, a transient and an outsider to this quarrel between Britain and America on the one hand and Russia on the other.

Experience. That is the word he would like to fall back on to justify himself to himself. The artist must taste all experience, from the noblest to the most degraded. Just as it is the artist's destiny to experience the most supreme creative joy, so he must be prepared to take upon himself all in life that is miserable, squalid, ignominious. It was in the name of experience that he underwent London – the dead days of IBM, the icy winter of 1962, one humiliating affair after another: stages in the poet's life, all of them, in the testing of his soul. Similarly Aldermaston – the wretched cubicle in which he works, with its plastic furniture and its view on to the back of a furnace, the armed man at his back – can be regarded simply as experience, as a further stage in his journey into the depths.

It is a justification that does not for a moment convince him. It is sophistry, that is all, contemptible sophistry. And if he is further going to claim that, just as sleeping with Astrid and her teddy-bear was getting to know moral squalor, so telling self-justifying lies to oneself is getting to know intellectual squalor at first hand, then the sophistry will only become more contemptible. There is nothing to be said for it; nor, to be ruthlessly honest, is there anything to be said for its having nothing to be said for it. As for ruthless honesty, ruthless honesty is not a hard trick to learn. On the contrary, it is the easiest thing in the world. As a poisonous toad is not poison to itself, so one soon develops a hard skin against one's own honesty. Death to reason, death to talk! All that matters is doing the right thing, whether for the right reason or the wrong reason or no reason at all.

Working out the right thing to do is not difficult. He does not need to think overlong to know what the right thing is. He could, if he chose, do the right thing with near infallible accuracy. What gives him pause is the question of whether he can go on being a poet while doing the right thing. When he tries to imagine what sort of poetry would flow from doing the right thing time after time after time, he sees only blank emptiness. The right thing is boring. So he is at an impasse: he would rather be bad than boring, has no respect for a person who would rather be bad than boring, and no respect either for the cleverness of being able to put his dilemma neatly into words.

Despite cricket and books, despite the ever-cheerful birds greeting the sunrise with chirrups from the apple-tree beneath his window, weekends remain hard to get through, particularly Sundays. He dreads waking up on Sunday mornings. There are rituals to help one through Sunday, principally going out and buying the newspaper and reading it on the sofa and clipping out the chess problems. But the newspaper will not take one much beyond eleven in the morning; and anyhow, reading the Sunday supplements is too transparently a way of killing time.

He is killing time, he is trying to kill Sunday so that Monday will come sooner, and with Monday the relief of work. But in a larger sense work is a way of killing time too. Everything he has done since he stepped ashore at Southampton has been a killing of time while he waits for his destiny to arrive. Destiny would not come to him in South Africa, he told himself; she would come (come like a bride!) only in London or Paris or perhaps Vienna, because only in the great cities of Europe does destiny reside. For nearly two years he waited and suffered in London, and destiny stayed away. Now, having not been strong enough to bear London, he has beaten a retreat into the countryside, a strategic retreat. Whether destiny pays visits to the countryside is not certain, even if it is the English countryside, and even if it is barely an hour by train from Waterloo.

Of course in his heart he knows destiny will not visit him unless he makes her do so. He has to sit down and write, that is the only way. But he cannot begin writing until the moment is right, and no matter how scrupulously he prepares himself, wiping the table clean, positioning the lamp, ruling a margin down the side of the blank page, sitting with his eyes shut, emptying his mind in readiness – in spite of all this, the words will not come to him. Or rather, many words will come, but not the right words, the sentence he will recognize at once, from its weight, from its poise and balance, as the destined one.

He hates these confrontations with the blank page, hates them to the extent of beginning to avoid them. He cannot bear the weight of despair that descends at the end of each fruitless session, the realization that again he has failed. Better not to wound oneself in this way, over and over. One might cease to be able to respond to the call when it comes, might become too weak, too abject.

He is well aware that his failure as a writer and his failure as a lover are so closely parallel that they might as well be the same thing. He is the man, the poet, the maker, the active principle, and the man is not supposed to wait for the woman's approach. On the contrary, it is the woman who is supposed to wait for the man. The woman is the one who sleeps until aroused by the prince's kiss; the woman is the bud that unfolds under the caress of the sun's rays. Unless he wills himself to act, nothing will happen, in love or in art. But he does not trust the will. Just as he cannot will himself to write but must wait for the aid of some force from outside, a force that used to be called the

Muse, so he cannot simply will himself to approach a woman without some intimation (from where? – from her? from within him? from above?) that she is his destiny. If he approaches a woman in any other spirit, the result is an entanglement like the wretched one with Astrid, an entanglement he was trying to escape from almost before it began.

There is another and more brutal way of saying the same thing. In fact there are hundreds of ways: he could spend the rest of his life listing them. But the most brutal way is to say that he is afraid: afraid of writing, afraid of women. He may pull faces at the poems he reads in *Ambit* and *Agenda*, but at least they are there, in print, in the world. How is he to know that the men who wrote them did not spend years squirming as fastidiously as he in front of the blank page? They squirmed, but then finally they pulled themselves together and wrote as best they could what had to be written, and mailed it out, and suffered the humiliation of rejection or the equal humiliation of seeing their effusions in cold print, in all their poverty. In the same way these men would have found an excuse, however lame, for speaking to some or other beautiful girl in the Underground, and if she turned her head away or passed a scornful remark in Italian to a friend, well, they would have found a way of suffering the rebuff in silence and the next day would have tried again with another girl. That is how it is done, that is how the world works. And one day they, these men, these poets, these lovers, would be lucky: the girl, no matter how exaltedly beautiful, would speak back, and one thing would lead to another and their lives would be transformed, both their lives, and that would be that. What more is required than a kind of stupid, insensitive doggedness, as lover, as writer, together with a readiness to fail and fail again?

What is wrong with him is that he is not prepared to fail.

He wants an A or an alpha or one hundred per cent for his every attempt, and a big *Excellent!* in the margin. Ludicrous! Childish! He does not have to be told so: he can see it for himself. Nevertheless. Nevertheless he cannot do it. Not today. Perhaps tomorrow. Perhaps tomorrow he will be in the mood, have the courage.

If he were a warmer person he would no doubt find it all easier: life, love, poetry. But warmth is not in his nature. Poetry is not written out of warmth anyway. Rimbaud was not warm. Baudelaire was not warm. Hot, indeed, yes, when it was needed – hot in life, hot in love – but not warm. He too is capable of being hot, he has not ceased to believe that. But for the present, the present indefinite, he is cold: cold, frozen.

And what is the upshot of this lack of heat, this lack of heart? The upshot is that he is sitting alone on a Sunday afternoon in an upstairs room in a house in the depths of the Berkshire countryside, with crows cawing in the fields and a grey mist hanging overhead, playing chess with himself, growing old, waiting for evening to fall so that he can with a good conscience fry his sausages and bread for supper. At eighteen he might have been a poet. Now he is not a poet, not a writer, not an artist. He is a computer programmer, a twenty-four-year-old computer programmer in a world in which there are no thirty-year-old computer programmers. At thirty one is too old to be a programmer: one turns oneself into something else – some kind of businessman – or one shoots oneself. It is only because he is young, because the neurons in his brain are still firing more or less infallibly, that he has a toehold in the British computer industry, in British society, in Britain itself. He and Ganapathy are two sides of the same coin: Ganapathy starving not because he is cut off from Mother India but because he doesn't eat properly, because despite his M.Sc. in computer science he doesn't know about vitamins and minerals and amino acids; and he locked into an attenuating endgame, playing himself, with each move, further into a corner and into defeat. One of these days the ambulance men will call at Ganapathy's flat and bring him out on a stretcher with a sheet over his face. When they have fetched Ganapathy they might as well come and fetch him too.